POSTMODERN MOVIES:

Neo-Comic Tragedies, Neo-Noirs, Neo-Westerns

Richard Gilmore

Theran Press

Theran Press is the academic publishing imprint of Silver Goat Media.

Theran is dedicated to authentic partnerships with our academic associates, to the quality design of ascholarly books, and to elite standards of peer review.

Theran seeks to free intellectuals from the confines of traditional publishing.

Theran scholars are authorities and revolutionaries in their respective fields.

Theran encourages new models for generating and distributing knowledge.

For our creatives. For our communities. For our world.

WWW.THERANPRESS.ORG

POSTMODERN MOVIES: NEO-COMIC TRAGEDIES, NEO-NOIRS, NEO-WESTERNS.
Copyright © 2016 by Richard Gilmore, All rights reserved.

Published by Silver Goat Media, LLC, Fargo, ND 58108. This publication is protected by copyright, and permission should be obtained from the publisher prior to any reproduction, storage in a retrieval system, or transmission in any form or by any means, electronic, mechanical, photocopying, recording, or likewise. SGM books are available at discounts, regardless of quantity, for K-12 schools, non-profits, or other educational institutions. To obtain permission(s) to use material from this work, or to order in bulk, please submit a written request to Silver Goat Media, LLC, PO Box 2336 Fargo, ND 58108, or contact SGM directly at: info@silvergoatmedia.com.

This book was designed and produced by Silver Goat Media, LLC. Fargo, ND U.S.A.
www.silvergoatmedia.com
SGM, the SGM goat, Theran Press, and the Theran theta are trademarks of Silver Goat Media.

Cover Design - Travis Klath © 2016
This book was typeset in TW Cen Mt & Gill Sans MT by Cady Ann Mittlestadt

ISBN-10: 194429600X
ISBN-13: 978-1944296001 (Silver Goat Media)

A portion of the proceeds from the sale of this book are donated to the Longspur Prairie Fund.
www.longspurprairie.org

2.0 - 170804

Printed and bound in the United States of America

POSTMODERN MOVIES:

Neo-Comic Tragedies, Neo-Noirs, Neo-Westerns

Richard Gilmore

THERAN PRESS

Contents

Acknowledgements ... i

Introduction ... iii

Neo-Tragic Comedies, Neo-Comic Tragedies

1 | *Raising Arizona* as an American Comedy and as a Comedy about America ... 3

2 | *No Country for Old Men*: The Coens' Tragic Western ... 23

Neo-Noirs

3 | The Dark Sublimity of *Chinatown* ... 49

4 | Economies of Time in Spike Lee's *Clockers* ... 67

5 | Art, Sex, and Time in Scorsese's *After Hours* ... 83

Neo-Westerns

6 | Regeneration through Stories and Song: The View from the Other Side of the West in Chris Eyre's *Smoke Signals* ... 109

7 | Bad Men at Play: On the Banality of Goodness in *Unforgiven* ... 127

Conclusions ... 143

Notes ... 147

Index ... 161

To my sister Lisa's sons
Emerson and Gillan,
my postmodern nephews

Acknowledgements

All of the essays in this book except the introduction and conclusion were previously published in volumes published by The University of Kentucky Press in their Philosophy of Popular Culture series edited by Mark T. Conard. "*Raising Arizona* as an American Comedy and as a Comedy about America" and "*No Country for Old Men*: The Coens' Tragic Western" were published in *The Philosophy of the Coen Brothers* edited by Mark T. Conard (Kentucky, 2009). "The Dark Sublimity of *Chinatown*" was published in *The Philosophy of Neo-Noir* edited by Mark T. Conard (Kentucky, 2007). "Economies of Time in *Clockers*" was published in *The Philosophy of Spike Lee* (Kentucky, 2011). "Art, Sex, and Time in Scorsese's *After Hours*" was published in *The Philosophy of Martin Scorsese* edited by Mark T. Conard (Kentucky, 2007). "Regeneration through Stories and Song: The View from the Other Side of the West in *Smoke Signals*" was published in *The Philosophy of the Western* edited by Jennifer McMahon and Steve Csaki (Kentucky, 2010). "Bad Men at Play: On the Banality of Goodness in *Unforgiven*" was published in *The Philosophy of Clint Eastwood* edited by Richard T. McClelland and Brian B. Clayton (Kentucky, 2014).

Introduction

"Postmodernism" is a term that goes back to the late 19th century, but for our purposes describes a social and cultural movement that emerges in the late 1960s and early 1970s. It means different things to different people. Most evidently, "postmodernism" signals a reaction against "modernism." Modernism is associated with the Enlightenment program of ever increasing knowledge by means of science, ever increasing social improvement because of technology, and ever increasing liberal and aesthetic sensitivity because of education. Modernism reflects a great deal of hope and optimism for the human race and the human project. Postmodernism is a reaction against that sense of confidence. I take Jean-François Lyotard's definition for my working understanding of the postmodern of it. Lyotard says, "I define *postmodern* as an incredulity toward metanarratives."[1] Lyotard's book, *The Postmodern Condition: A Report on Knowledge,* was published in 1979, and so postmodernism can be taken as a fully emerged cultural movement by then. A "metanarrative" is a dominating ideological structure. Christianity is a metanarrative. Science, as it functions as a social concept, is a metanarrative. Capitalism is a metanarrative. Democracy is a metanarrative. Modernism is about trusting the metanarratives. It is about trusting their reliability and their truth. "An incredulity toward metanarratives" is about no longer trusting the metanarratives. It is about being suspicious of all metanarratives. It reads metanarratives primarily as vectors of power, and so critically looks to see who benefits from a particular metanarrative, rather than just trusting in the truth of the metanarratives one is born into.

In literary theory, the process of revealing the instability of metanarratives was undertaken by means of showing the instability of meaning in any and every text. The master of this was Jacques Derrida. His method was called "deconstruction." A text is constructed to display a specific meaning. Modernism, in art, involved discovering the true meaning of a text or painting or sculpture or any artwork. Deconstruction, on the other hand, is devoted to showing how every artwork generates multiple meanings, and no final true interpretation can ever be found.

I will not be deconstructing artworks, but I am fascinated by the way artworks work to deconstruct their own metanarratives. I take the metanarrative of an artwork to be—at least one of an artwork's metanarratives—a genre.

Derrida, in his essay "The Law of Genre," I won't say deconstructs, but he severely problematizes the issue of genre. First of all, as he points out, genre is based on *repetition*.[2] You cannot have a genre of one example of something. The very concept of a genre is based on some characteristic or characteristics that are shared among a number of examples. A characteristic repeated among a number of examples is what makes a genre a genre. The thing about repetition, however, is that it is rarely, if ever, perfect. Change 'insinuates' itself into virtually every repetition.[3] This creates the paradox of genre. On the one hand, "as soon as genre announces itself, one must respect a norm, one must not cross a line of demarcation, one must not risk impurity, anomaly, or monstrosity."[4] On the other hand, in repetition, anomalies, impurities, and monstrosities naturally, inescapably, occur. Derrida poses the conclusion of this paradox as a question: "What if there were, lodged within the heart of the law [of genre] itself, a law of impurity or a principle of contamination? And suppose the condition for the possibility of the law were the a priori of a counter-law, an axiom of impossibility that would confound its sense, order, and reason?"[5]

This idea that within the heart of the law of genre, within the heart of any particular genre, there is a counter-law, a principle of impurity and contamination, which means that every member of a genre also, in some sense, does not belong to the genre. This is the paradox. This paradox invokes the sorites paradox, also known as the paradox of the heap (from the Greek *soros* meaning 'heap'). The paradox of the heap is very simple. If there is a heap of sand and you remove one grain of sand, there is still a heap of sand. There is no condition under which you can remove one grain of sand and convert a heap into a non-heap. Yet, if you keep removing grains of sand, there will not only be no heap there, there will be no sand left at all. The sorites paradox works in the other direction as well: if you have one grain of sand and add a grain of sand to it, it is not a heap. There is no condition, no number of grains of sand, under which you can add one grain of sand and convert a non-heap into a heap. And yet, if you keep adding grains of sand, at some point, there will definitely be a heap of sand there.

The sorites paradox is understood to be a paradox of vagueness. A heap is a vague term. There are aggregates that are clearly not heaps, and there are aggregates that are clearly heaps, and then there are aggregates that are ambiguous, not quite not a heap, but not quite a heap either. Bertrand Russell calls the area of maxim vagueness the "penumbra."[6] There is an aggregate of grains of sand, but you could just as accurately call it a heap as a non-heap. The thing about the sorites paradox is that all concepts, all words are subject to some degree of vagueness. Sometimes it depends on what you mean by "is." Take the example of a swizzle stick, generally a fairly unambiguous item. If someone were to remove one molecule from a particular swizzle stick, would that object continue to be a swizzle stick? The answer is an unambiguous "Yes." If this act is repeated, however, one molecule removed at a time, at some point what will remain will not look anything like, nor serve the function of, a swizzle stick. There is no one step in the process of removal when the swizzle stick became a non-swizzle stick, but at some point one is pressed to say that what remains is no longer a swizzle stick.[7]

Genres, as Derrida is pointing out, have an inherent vagueness at their core. Consider the first movie with a cowboy and some horses. It is not yet a western because the genre of the western has not been identified yet. A second movie is made. It too has a cowboy and some horses, but whereas the first movie involved robbing a bank, the second movie involved a cattle drive. On the one hand, one might want to say that these are two very different genres, the first is a crime movie, the second is a work story. The next movie with a cowboy and some horses involves a man arriving in a new town and developing a love interest with the local Madame. Again, a very different genre of movie, this time a love story or romantic drama. These will all emerge, eventually, as classic westerns, but that is not at all obvious from the outset. This pattern continues with each new example. Is *McCabe & Mrs. Miller* (Robert Altman, 1971) a western? In some ways, it does not look like a western at all. The look of the movie is very stylized.

The stars (Warren Beatty and Julie Christie) are not typical western actors. The story is complicated and modern. In other ways, it is obviously a western: it takes place in the west, in a frontier town, and there are horses and cowboys.

This is what philosophy does. It makes things complicated. It is a basic intuition of philosophy that things are more complicated than we think they are. For most people, most of the time, genres are pretty stable, reliable things. A western is a western. A romantic comedy is a romantic comedy. There is, however, always a penumbra, an area of vagueness.

Philosophy is generally interested in these areas of vagueness. Why? Why care about the marginal cases? There are several reasons. One reason is predictive. If you have a fixed concept about who a person is, for example, and do not recognize any ambiguity in their character, then you will be surprised, perhaps even shocked, when they behave in ways that do not fit your fixed model and expectations. If you have a more open view of another person, that includes an appreciation for ambiguities in their character, you will be able to better anticipate what they will do and will be able to work more easily with any new behaviors that do emerge.

A second reason is emancipatory. We can become locked into certain views or conceptions of how the world is in a way that can imprison us conceptually. Sometimes we need to think outside the box. On the other hand, sometimes we are really confused and can see no stability or any reliable way to make sense of a situation. Philosophy is sometimes concerned with ambiguating a concept or situation. That means when people are making assumptions about a situation or a concept with complete certainty, they sometimes will be helped if they can be freed from their assumptions, if their assumptions are problematized in some way, or the ambiguity in their assumptions is made clear to them. For example, a person has a concept of what it means to be married, and say their idea of a legitimate marriage is between a man and a woman. Then they discover a friend of theirs is married, but to someone of the same sex. A lot of cognitive and emotional dissonance can ensue from this situation. What may be needed is for their concept of marriage to be ambiguated, enlarged in a way to accommodate this new situation that they have encountered in the world.

Some other times, just the opposite movement is needed: a concept or situation needs to be disambiguated. If we continue with the gay marriage example, the first step is ambiguating the concept of marriage, but the second step is disambiguating a new concept of marriage, a new definition of what constitutes a legitimate marriage. This is in fact happening, with new laws being made to accommodate widespread public sentiment about the injustice of the old law, but we will also need a new, clear description of what will constitute a legal marriage. It may be that same sex marriages are legitimate, but not marrying your pet or your plant. Sometimes we need to be freed conceptually by means of recognizing the inherent ambiguity in some concept that we have, and sometimes we need to find some way out of an ambiguous quagmire, to find some stable conceptual clarity to move forward. That will be the source of freedom.

A final reason that the areas of maxim ambiguity are of interest to philosophers is because they are the most interesting conceptual places *simplicitur*. Sometimes you just want to watch a very standard, predictable western. Just watching episode after episode of *Bonanza*, however, can get pretty boring. The westerns that really make us think will be those westerns that maximally problematize the genre. John Ford's *The Searchers* (1956) was a radical and disturbing western, as is Clint Eastwood's *Unforgiven* (1992). These are both unquestionably westerns, and yet they strongly disturb some classic characteristics of the genre of the western. In the classic western, the main protagonist is a white-hat-wearing good guy. Neither Ethan Edwards (John Wayne) nor William Munny (Clint Eastwood) are even remotely good guys. Ethan Edwards is a racist, violent murderer. William Munny is, when he drinks, a violent psychopath.

This raises two questions. First, why make such a genre-disturbing movie? And second, why philosophize about it? The basic answer is the same as above: we have ideas that seem to us reliable and certain, but are in one way or another limiting us conceptually. The classic westerns were always racist and they celebrated violence. We (and here I mean primarily white, non-tribal, bourgeois types like me) watch them unreflectively and with pleasure without realizing how they are reinforcing certain stereotypes—negative stereotypes—about how the world is and how we should be in the world. Watching a typical western, we do not see how our own negative stereotypes are being developed and reinforced. John Ford makes a western with a main protagonist, Ethan Edwards, that makes explicit what has always remained implicit: the racism and violence of western protagonists.

Ethan Edwards performs a function that Stanley Fish has called being "surprised by sin." Fish talks about "sin" because he is using Milton's *Paradise Lost* as his example and Milton was very much concerned with the problematic of sin. I am not so much concerned with sin as with the conceptual deformities that imprison or impede us. The dynamic of being surprised by sin functions like this: The artist, say Milton, creates a character that is somehow very compelling, maybe even the most compelling character in the artwork, and then, at a crucial moment, dramatically emphasizes a negative characteristic of the character. It will be a characteristic that we may have seen all along, but we have been unwilling to acknowledge because we liked the character so much. The character we are drawn to in *Paradise Lost*, as Fish points out, is Satan. Satan is central to the narrative and we begin to identify with his struggles and plans. We come to respect his intelligence and a certain kind of integrity he possesses. When he explicitly and openly defies God, we are surprised not by his sin so much as our own. We should have known that Satan was not the figure we should be identifying with all along. What we are surprised by is our own complicity with a thing that, in another part of our thinking, we fully disapprove of. As Fish says, "Milton's method is to re-create in the mind of the reader…the drama of the Fall…."[8]

Few would admit to or acknowledge being a racist, but watching classic westerns we often feel great unreflective pleasure when the protagonist kills a number of Indians. What the artist is doing, John Ford as much as Milton, is making us explicitly aware of our own deepest commitments and ashamed of our passing complicity with certain social prejudices we would explicitly abhor.

Artists and artworks, in this way, can free us from our own unreflective tendencies to engage in practices we would reflectively avoid. This helps us to be more consistently our selves, and frees us from conceptual traps that we can fall into. It also severely disrupts genre categories. We need the ambiguating disruptive instantiation of the genre for these practical and moral reasons. Philosophy is good for making these functions of genre disruptive examples more explicit and for making clear what lessons we can learn from these particular examples.

Getting back to Derrida and what he calls "the law of the law of genre." This is how he defines the law, along with some additional exposition:

> It is precisely a principle of contamination, a law of impurity, a parasitical economy. In the code of set theories, if I may use it at least figuratively, I would speak of a sort of participation without belonging—a taking part in without being a part of, without having membership in a set. With the inevitable dividing of the trait that marks membership, the boundary of the set comes to form, by invagination, an internal pocket larger than the whole; and the outcome of this division and of this abounding remains as singular as it is limitless.[9]

Picture a circle with one section of its curvature interrupted by another slightly larger circle, which has an outer rim that is interrupted by another slightly larger circle, ad infinitum. The original circle is an established genre. The slightly larger circle that interrupts the completion of that original circle is, as it were, a neo-form of the original genre. It is a neo-form, but also a natural part of and an extension of, the original genre. The boundary of a genre, which is what the circles mark, represents the place of maximum ambiguity. It is penumbral. It contains examples that at once do and do not fit within the genre set.

Derrida uses the surprising neologism/metaphor/image of "invagination" to describe this phenomenon at the boundary edge of a genre. It is the interruption of the completion of the genre boundary by an "internal pocket larger than the whole." "Invagination" suggests the fertile, generative nature of this pocket. It reproduces the original genre in an entirely new form. Derrida speaks of the "taxonomic exuberance" and the "fertile proliferation" that the concept of genre produces.[10] It is in the nature of a genre that almost anything can be made to fit into any collection of items, any genre, with enough imagination and wit to make the case for its inclusion. *Thelma & Louise* (Ridley Scott, 1991) can be categorized as a modernized, feminized western. Two outlaws are on the run from the law. Their guilt or innocence is ambiguous to us, but not to the increasingly large number of lawmen out to get them. The landscape is the west. Their horses are the horsepower of a car, but it functions in essentially the same way as traditional western horses. It takes place in contemporary times, but the basic narrative is almost identical to George Roy Hill's *Butch Cassidy and the Sundance Kid* (1969) — a film that no one would dispute was a western - although, in its own way, it is quite unconventional as a western and is certainly a neo-western. The biggest "problem" with *Thelma & Louise* for the genre of the western is that the two protagonists are women, but once you get past that, it fits quite nicely into the western genre, or rather, into the invaginated pocket at the boundary of the concept of a western that opens up all sorts of other new possibilities to be included in the western genre.

Derrida is a philosopher and he is doing what philosophers always do. He is focusing on a particular area of our conceptual landscape, in this case on the nature of genre and, first of all, he is problematizing it, ambiguating it. That is, he is drawing out inherent ambiguities in our use of the concept of a genre that we had not seen before. After ambiguating the concept of genre, he then searches for some kind of conceptual clarity that helps us to move forward with the now enlarged concept of genre and its more fertile application in the world. Now we can see the concept of genre not as a fixed, closed, almost as it were pre-determined category, but as a flexible, fertile, illimitable possibility for reading new movies.

The chapters of this work fall into three sections: Neo-Comedies/Tragedies, Neo-Noirs, Neo-Westerns. The concept of the "neo" genre refers to precisely the invaginated, penumbral pockets at the edge of a genre. It is the area, as I have been arguing, of maximum ambiguity with respect to belonging to a genre, but also the space of maximum fertility, generative power, and philosophical potential.

In the first section, I consider two movies by the Coen brothers, *Raising Arizona* (1987) and *No Country for Old Men* (2007). At the end of the dialogue *Symposium*, Plato has Apollodorus, who is narrating the story of a group of speeches that were presented at a drinking party some years before, a drinking party attended by Socrates, describe the final scene of the party. Everyone has left the party or passed out from too much wine except Socrates, Agathon, and Aristophanes. Apollodorus says, "Socrates was trying to prove to them that authors should be able to write both comedy and tragedy: the skillful tragic dramatist should also be a comic poet."[11] This is a perfect description of the Coen brothers who are masters of both comedy and tragedy and often work simultaneously in both, producing comic tragedies and tragic comedies. I consider *Raising Arizona* and *No Country for Old Men* to both occupy this liminal, penumbral area of being simultaneously comedy and tragedy. The tragedy of *Raising Arizona* is in the inability to have a child of H. I. McDunnough (Nicolas Cage) and Edwina 'Ed' McDunnough (Holly Hunter) and from the perspective of Nathan and Florence Arizona (T. J. Kuhn and Lynne Kitei) who lose one of their children. The rest is all comedy, but there is a distinct tragic undertow to all of the wild comedy. *No Country for Old Men* is almost pure tragedy. The comedy lies almost entirely in the haircut worn by Anton Chigurh (Javier Bardem), but it is a very significant bit of comedy that pervades the inevitability of the tragedy. That this emissary of death should look faintly ridiculous is a deep commentary on the nature of what frightens us most.

The second section is on neo-noirs and consists of one classic neo-noir, *Chinatown* (Polanski, 1974), and two very marginal-as-noirs movies, *After Hours* (Scorsese, 1985) and *Clockers* (Lee, 1995). Each of these movies consists of a narrative from the underside of urban life, which is very noir. Each has, as a protagonist, a character that is flawed, but persistent, which is very noir. There is crime, murder, unorthodox sexual relations in all three, all very noir. Only *Chinatown* has Venetian blinds, but windows play a significant role in all three movies.

The third section contains two essays on two movies that I am calling neo-westerns. *Smoke Signals* (Eyre, 1998) is clearly a radically new kind of western; a western from the perspective of American Indians, but it reproduces some classic western themes: the themes of fathers (bad) and sons (good), the theme of the encounter between White People and Native People, the theme of trying to find one's way home. The final film I look at is Clint Eastwood's *Unforgiven*. It is a revisionist western, especially in the way it portrays violence. The classic western tends to portray violence as heroic and redemptive. In *Unforgiven*, the violence is horrific and shocking and in no way redemptive. No forgiveness is given. To call all of these films "neo" versions of their respective genres is just to highlight how innovative and radical they are. Each in its own way is representative of its genre as well.

Section One

Neo-Tragic Comedies

Neo-Comic Tragedies

1 | *Raising Arizona* as an American Comedy

We grew up in America, and we tell American stories in American settings within American frames of reference....

– Ethan Coen in an interview

Our American literature and spiritual history are...in the optative mood....

– Ralph Waldo Emerson, "The Transcendentalist"

Raising Arizona (1987) begins with what sounds like the slamming shut of prison doors. It is, to be sure, an ominous sound, and proleptic in at least two ways. First, it anticipates the sound that our protagonist is about to hear within minutes of our first meeting him, and second, it anticipates one of the major themes of the movie which is, in the words of Ethan Coen, "family life versus being an outlaw."[14] That is, presumably, to the outlaw, family life can seem like some prison doors swung shut. Immediately following the sound of the slamming-shut prison doors there is banjo music and an image of what we learn is a police height measure for photographing arrested criminals. A young man (Nicolas Cage) is thrown into the point of view of the camera so that we can take his measure against the height chart. In a voice-over, we hear "My name is H. I. McDunnough. Call me Hi." I understand Hi's name (constructed anagrammatically from his first two initials) to suggest a spatial metaphor, a description of his ambitions, which are, I want to say, very American ambitions. The banjo music in the background is Pete Seeger's "Goofing Off Suite," which, like America itself, is a fascinating medley of American folk music, motifs from high European classical music (Bach and Beethoven), Russian folk music, and even yodeling.[15]

Hi is the main protagonist of the film and provides the voice-over narration that accompanies the regular narrative of the film. Although Hi is the main protagonist, it is Ed (Holly Hunter), short for Edwina, who establishes the agon, with her strong sense of what she wants and what constitutes natural justice. She is in this way sort of like Antigone, except in this case, the natural justice takes the form of stealing a live baby from a family that, it could be argued, have too many, rather than burying one's dead brother against the laws of the state.

"Goofing off" pretty much describes the sense one gets of what the Coens are doing in the opening sequence of the movie. There is one disjunctive discontinuity after another, each one constituting a kind of slapstick joke, and yet each one reverberates with a deeper truth. There is the overall structural discontinuity between Hi's voice-over narration and what we see him doing. Hi sounds, in the voice-over, like he speaks from a place of detached, even philosophical, wisdom, but what we actually see him doing shows him to be a not-very-bright, repeat offender, petty criminal with an enthusiasm for robbing convenience stores. That disjunction is kind of funny. His enthusiasm for robbing convenience stores is kind of funny in itself, as is his evident incompetence at it, which is why he goes to jail so often, as his acceptance of jail time is, as it were, just part of life, of his life anyway. That he uses his time between crimes, his time being booked for the crimes he has committed, to woo Ed, who is a police officer and the photographer for his mug shots, is funny and ridiculous. Their marriage, "starter home," "salad days," infertility, despair, and kidnapping scheme are all a little ridiculous, and yet, even though they are presented as, basically, funny, there is a sort of underlying truth to all of it. America does have a kind of fascination-love affair with the image of the outlaw, so choosing to be an outlaw is not really that crazy. And it is hard starting a family in this modern world, even if—or especially if—you are an outlaw by trade. And starter homes sometimes are little mobile homes in the desert. And sometimes, in spite of your best efforts, nature does not cooperate, and infertility may happen.

When Hi says, "I tried to stand up and fly straight, but it wasn't easy with that sumbitch Reagan in the White House...I dunno, they say he is a decent man, so...maybe his advisers are confused."[16]   It is such a mish mash of deep political wisdom, weird folksy compassion, and just raw, self-serving excuse that it is hard to find one's way with it. It is funny and true and kind of crazy all at the same time. It also has a vaguely socialist ring to it, and, of course, Pete Seeger, the creator of the music we are hearing in the background, the "Goofing Off Suite," was a famous socialist and defender of the people, which further suggests some deeper political message behind the craziness. This, one might say, quoting the American poet Robert Frost, is "play for mortal stakes."[17]

The Optative Mood and America

We, in America, are weaned on the milk of aspiration. This is what I understand Emerson to mean when he describes our spiritual history as being in the "optative mood." "Optative" means expressing a desire or a wish or a hope. An optative mood is a mood of aspiration. The great advantage of this spiritual history is the energy and the inventiveness it calls forth in American people. The downside is that our ethos is so forward looking, so much depends on each individual making something of himself or herself out of their own energy, out of their own selves, that not much is given. We do not inherit an identity as much as find ourselves tasked with (to use a Coen expression from *Fargo*) creating an identity. That is an easier task for some than for others, and certainly there are some deep deceptions in the American mythos of self-creation, deceptions about the irrelevance of the conditions of one's birth, of the role of social class or money or race. So, on the one hand, we have more freedom than most in history to make of ourselves what we will. On the other hand, that puts a considerable burden on each of us as individuals to come up with a unique self to be.

American Exceptionalism

Part of the American mythos, part of the sense of what is especially unique about America, is captured in the idea of 'American Exceptionalism.' This idea is usually traced back to Tocqueville's *Democracy in America* (1862), but it can be found in an even earlier version in a famous sermon given by John Winthrop in 1630 in which he describes a future of America that "…wee will be seen as a citty upon a hill."[18] This expression of American Exceptionalism, of a future America as "a city upon a hill," is aspirational in at least two ways. It is aspirational in the sense that it is describing a hoped-for state of the country that can be achieved if we are true to certain principles, it describes what we should aspire to for our future country, it expresses a dream of what America could be. It is also aspirational in the sense that this hoped-for state, once achieved, will itself represent an aspirational goal to the rest of the world.

This idea of there being something special about America, something not just unique but also superior, the idea of America as an idea of some kind of better possibility, seems to pervade our thinking about ourselves, as well as the thinking of others about us, and is—as most things are—a blessing and a curse. The blessing is the way the idea of America's exceptionalism empowers us to pursue our own dreams of what we want to be. It is part of the American ideal that we are not necessarily limited by birth or class or race. On the other hand, the expectations of individual achievement are very high and we often fail to measure up. It is not an incidental detail, I think, that the first image we see of Hi is of him thrown against a height measure, which, under the circumstances—he is being measured for an arrest photo in a police station—indicates a certain failure to measure up to the high expectations of society.

Comedy

Raising Arizona is a comedy.[19] I take it to be a comedy in at least two senses. First it is a comedy because it is very funny. The second way that I see *Raising Arizona* as a comedy is in the classic sense of a comedy—which derives from Aristotle's definition of a comedy[20]—as a narrative that begins in a bad place but, in its narrative unfolding, ends in a good place. This is why Dante's narrative of a descent into hell and subsequent journey through purgatory and paradise is called *The Divine Comedy*.[21] It is not so much that it is a humorous work, although there are some very funny passages in it, but because it follows the classic trajectory of a comedy as described by Aristotle.

This claim, that *Raising Arizona* is a comedy in this classic sense, depends on an interpretation of the ending of the movie as being an affirmation of a better future for Hi and Ed. The ending of the movie seems to be ambiguous. Hi is having another one of his dreams (although all of his previous dreams in the movie have turned out to be connected with reality) and he is dreaming of a better and more fruitful future, but their actual situation seems to be worse: they are baby-less, and Ed has pronounced, in her definitive way, their (Hi's and Ed's) complete unsuitableness to each other and her determination to leave him. Whether they stay together or not remains undetermined by the narrative of the movie. To affirm the movie as a having the form of a classic comedy means finding in this very ambiguity some kind of affirmation that transcends the early hopefulness and excitement of their original courtship and marriage.

Raising Hi

I interpret the title of the movie, *Raising Arizona*, to indicate the most fundamental theme of the movie: namely, the aspirational theme of self-improvement that is so central to the American identity. The basic trope is the idea of height, so I take Hi's name to be a kind of spatial metaphor of his aspirations. What constitutes growth, what constitutes the necessary change in condition, from a worse to a better condition (so that the movie can fulfill the form of a comedy), will be a change in one's aspirations. At the beginning of the movie, I take Hi's aspirations to be relatively uncomplicated. What he wanted to be was also what he was, an outlaw. The outlaw is a kind of American aspiration, an American ideal. The outlaw is just an extreme form of the American ideal of the frontiersman, the adventurer, the one who braves the wilderness and does so because of too much wildness still in him or her. The classic American movie genre of the Western is filled with figures that straddle the line between law and lawlessness, so that the good Westerner is just barely across the line on the side of the law, and the only one wild enough to go after the bad Westerner is the one who has slipped to the far side of the law and into a lawless wildness. The connection with the American movie genre of the Western is made explicit with some allusions to westerns in *Raising Arizona*, for example, the location of the film in the Southwest, the long-coat dusters worn by Gale (John Goodman) and Evelle (William Forsythe) when they rob the bank, and the showdown between Hi and Leonard Smalls (Randall "Tex" Cobb).

Identity

The problem of creating an identity for oneself can be framed in terms of the relationship between universals (or generals) and particulars. That is, to be something is to participate in some form of a universal: one is a lawyer or a teacher or a fifth grader or an American. But to participate too much in a universal, to identify oneself too deeply with a general idea, is to lack any particular identity at all.[22] On the other hand, to be too idiosyncratically particular is, in a way, also to lack an identity. It is to have no continuous identity at all. We construct our identities, therefore, out of a combination of some kind of general or universal idea inflected by our own particular characteristics. In part, our particularity is constituted by just the particular array of general ideas that we participate in, so one way to develop one's identity is in choosing which combination of general ideas in which to participate. A way to improve one's identity is to, somehow, improve on the complex array of universals that we participate in, making them all more harmonious or more beautiful or maybe just more complex.

Of course, we do not have a choice about many of the universals that we participate in, or not much of a choice. We do not choose (for the most part) our gender, whether we will be born rich or poor, in the Northeast or the Southwest. It seems clear that we make some choices, and it will be in those choices that such identity as we can make we do make.

Hi, at the beginning of *Raising Arizona*, has what seems to be a fairly simple identity structure. He seems to identify himself as an outlaw. He blames Reagan (or his advisors) for his outlaw ways, but that really seems to be more a function of his outlaw ways than a real explanation of them. (When he really wants a job, he seems to have no trouble getting one. When he wants a paper, he prefers to steal it than to pay the thirty five cents, and that seems to be a matter of preference and principle rather than need.) The life of an outlaw is a kind of "primitive," pre-Christian, pre-capitalist kind of existence. It is lived in the present moment much more than toward any particular future. It is cyclical, like the seasons. There is the excitement of doing the crime, and then the over-structured time of being in jail, then back to the crime and back to jail. As Hi says, "Now I don't know how you come down on the incarceration question, whether it's for rehabilitation or revenge. But I was beginning to think that revenge is the only argument that makes any sense."[23] We hear this voice-over as we watch Hi commit another crime after just seeing him let out of jail. Furthermore, we see that he has pretty much botched this crime by accidentally locking himself out of his car and the signs (we hear a police siren in the distance) indicate that he will soon be back in the slammer. So his perspective pretty much mirrors his reality *viz a viz* the incarceration question. Rehabilitation does not seem to be a part of the system, at least if Hi is the example.

In a sense, however, these simple primitive cycles and his relatively simple identity structure are already, for Hi, on their way to being things of the past and they become that in, as it were, the blink of an eye. Heidegger speaks of how the possibility of a new encounter, a new way of encountering the world will occur to us in the blink of an eye (an *Augenblick* in Heidegger's German).[24] The French philosopher, Alain Badiou, talks about a similar phenomenon as an "event."[25] An "event" is something that happens that does not quite fit into our established system of knowledge, and so it will appear to us as something unaccountable, something that we cannot quite get our minds around even as we recognize the great importance of the encounter. Badiou identifies four realms, four general categories, of events: politics, science, art, and love.[26] If we consider the final category, then, an event in love will be an encounter with another person which, as it were, opens up possibilities to us that we had never understood were possibilities, it creates a disturbance for us that we do not quite know how to quell. We will always be tempted, in the presence of an event, to turn away from the event, to pretend it did not happen, because the event is always experienced as being beyond us, beyond what we have the capabilities for. Ethics, for Badiou, is about having the courage to be true to, to be faithful to, the event.

The Event

I take it that the flash of light from the flashbulb when Ed first takes Hi's photograph in the lineup at the beginning of the movie to signal, as well, the occurrence of an event. What is the event? If Hi's identity is constituted according to the general idea of the outlaw, Ed's identity seems to be constituted primarily in terms of the law. Her cold-sounding, apparently indifferent, and oft repeated "Turn to the right!" is a kind of pure expression of the law. In that flash of a light, however, a mutual recognition seems to occur. Hi and Ed see in each other the possibility of another narrative, another way of being that would supplement and reconstitute their present ways, and in ways that neither quite understands, but for which both feel an attraction and a need.

Indeed, their marriage generates such a powerful sense of love for both of them during what Hi refers to as "the salad days" of their marriage that they felt, in Hi's words expressing Ed's feelings, "that there was too much love and beauty for just the two of us and every day we kept a child out of the world was a day he might later regret having missed."[27] They feel, I want to say, the great potential of their marriage, but do not yet understand how to unleash the power of this potential. The anti-law, joy-in-the-moment life of the outlaw has no future, and the pure form of the law is itself barren. The rocky road that Hi and Ed have to follow, then, is the road from the unworkable antinomy of trying to combine in their pure forms outlaw and law, to a way of finding, for each, the virtue of the other that will unleash the potential powers of both. That is, Hi has to learn the value of law, and Ed the value of ad hoc life in the moment in a way that makes a shared future that they can aspire to together possible.

The plot of the movie is all about the beginning of this journey. The beginning of this journey turns out to be quite funny. Perhaps it should not be, involving as it does, a recidivist criminal offender, the kidnapping of an infant, a brutal "warthog from hell" biker who kills small animals with indiscriminate zeal, two escaped criminals, among other miscreants and malfeasance. Yet, as bad as a description of the characters and acts involved sound, what we feel for these characters doing these things is, as Georg Sesslen says, "tenderness."[28]

Plato on Two Kinds of Laughter

This leads me to Plato's, not exactly explicit, theory of humor. In book seven of Plato's *Republic*, in the section known as the allegory of the cave, Plato describes two different kinds of laughter.[29] The first kind of laughter he describes is the laughter of the people who are trapped inside the cave, the people who take mere shadows for reality. They laugh at the people who return to the cave from outside because when those people return from out of the bright light of reality back into the darkness of the cave, they stumble around, blinded by the darkness of the cave. To those inside the cave, those whose eyes are used to the darkness, this stumbling around looks like incompetence, and the people inside the cave think it is hysterically funny to see such bumbling. The second kind of laughter, however, is quite different. The second form of laughter is the laughter of the people outside the cave as they watch each new person who escapes from the cave and tries to walk in the bright light of day (reality) before their eyes have gotten used to all of the light. They stumble too and this makes the people whose eyes are now used to the light laugh. On the surface, these two forms of laughter seem quite similar, but, in reality, they are completely different. What is the difference? The difference is that the first kind of laughter is a laughter of ridicule, of supposed superiority at the expense of a supposed inferior. It is a laughter that separates and makes other. The second kind of laughter is like the laughter of parents seeing their child take her or his first wobbly step. It is a laughter of joy and love and inclusion. It is a laughter that welcomes and bonds.

Jokes

Raising Arizona is full of jokes. Some of the jokes are explicit. Although Hi woos Ed with a joke about a tipped cement mixer and some escaped hardened criminals (a joke Ed had heard before), most of the explicit jokes are of the 'bad laughter' variety, and they are told by Glen (Sam McMurray). The rest of the jokes in the movie are implicit. They are not presented explicitly as jokes, but if you see them as jokes, they are quite funny, and also, generally, more or less tender. In a way, they include us and affirm our shared humanity rather than exclude us or reinforce a sense of our otherness. Ted Cohen, in his book called *Jokes: Philosophical Thoughts on Joking Matters*, describes the purpose of jokes in terms of "relief from certain oppressions, and the attainment of a very special kind of intimacy."[30] With jokes, one has to do some work, do some thinking. Frequently, jokes work by ellipsis, something is left out that has to be supplied by the hearer. So, at first, the missing element occurs as just a sort of puzzling *non sequitur*, then, you get it and see how the missing piece solves the puzzle. The result is an intimacy based on a shared understanding, based on "the sense held mutually by teller and hearer that they are joined in feeling."[31] So, the philosophical importance of jokes has to do with the way they free us from things that oppress us, by giving us a certain distance, a certain detached perspective on those things, and the way they foster intimacy and community between the teller and the hearer of the joke.

In a movie like *Raising Arizona*, the implicit jokes are frequently signaled only by an oddness, and one may laugh at them without being fully aware of what is funny, as though we got the joke subconsciously, if not quite fully consciously. Hi's enthusiastic and energetic seduction of Ed from the position of the one who is being booked and sent to jail is funny because it is a very odd situation in which to begin a seduction, since the very fact that one is a convicted criminal would seem to disqualify one as an appropriate partner, especially for a police officer. The tenderness, the good laughter of these sequences, resides in the way that it is in the nature of wooing to be, to feel, more or less unworthy, and yet we do it anyway. There is always something suspicious about wooing, a question of reliability and of motives that shadows every wooer with a taint of criminality. The wooer understands this as well as the wooed, and yet we woo and are wooed. From inside the process all of this causes anxiety, from outside, it looks kind of funny. It is funny that Hi tells Ed that her ex-fiancé knows where to find him, "…in the Munroe County Maximum Security Correctional Facility for Men, State Farm Road Number Thirty-One; Tempe, Arizona," since it is at once gallant and ridiculous. It is funny the way words work as things outside of us, with a kind of logic of their own that can be confounding, the way "Well, okay then" can be the words that set Hi free by the head of the parole board, and the identical words can work to make him married. It is funny the way, when someone says, "You're not just tellin' us what we wanna hear?" and you say, "No sir, no way." And then they say "'Cause we just wanna hear the truth," and you think, well, I am telling the truth, and so you say, "Well then I guess I am tellin' you what you wanna hear." Then they say, "Boy, didn't we just tell you not to do that?" Okay then. I hate it when that happens.

All of these jokes seem to be doing just what Ted Cohen says about jokes. In our laughter at these scenes we feel ourselves getting some distance from, and some perspective on, the kinds of things that cause us anxiety and oppress us. In our laughter, we feel a certain tenderness for Hi and Ed, and maybe even for Dot (Frances McDormand) and Glen, as well as for ourselves, and this feeling of tenderness is a feeling of a kind of intimacy with these characters. If we are in a movie theater, and our laughter is shared by others in the audience, this feeling of intimacy and shared feeling, shared community, is created in the actual movie theater itself.

There is, at least one, Freudian joke in the movie: the way the gynecologist (Ralph Norton) is using his cigar—what Freud would call a phallic symbol—as a pointer to the diagram of a woman's reproductive system. In the way he manipulates the cigar against the diagram he seems to be simultaneously explaining the problem of Ed's infertility and simulating sex. This is a doctor joke, a Freudian joke, and a joke on Freud (who famously said "Sometimes a cigar is just a cigar" and died, tragically, of mouth cancer, suggesting that the great psychologist was not entirely in control of his own psyche).

Polysemousness

A narrative that has multiple levels of meaning can be called polysemous. Polysemous not only characterizes the scene with the gynecologist, but is characteristic of *Raising Arizona* as a whole. Dante, in his famous letter to Can Grande, describes how his *Commedia* is polysemous. Dante says that each scene in the *Commedia* has four levels of meaning: first, the literal narrative, then the allegorical meaning, then the moral meaning, and finally the anagogical meaning of the scene. For example, the *Commedia* begins:

> Midway in our life's journey, I went astray
> from the straight road and woke to find myself
> alone in a dark wood....[32]

The four levels of interpretation for this opening scene would be, first, that, literally, the narrator, Dante, was sleepwalking and woke up after having veered off the road he had meant to be on and was now lost in a dark wood. The allegorical meaning is that this is a thing that has happened to virtually everyone, and that many of us are, too, lost in a dark wood (of sin and error). The moral significance has to do with the recognition of this fact of our lostness and the need to recover our moral bearings and that the subsequent story may help us with this. The anagogical meaning is that this is not just a practical moral problem, but also a spiritual problem, and that our lostness is not just a reflection of our being out of sync with our own moral convictions, but that we are also out of sync with the universe as whole, or with God, and that dire steps must be taken to remedy this dire condition.

Although the Coen brothers do not claim this kind of polysemous content for *Raising Arizona* as explicitly as Dante does for his *Commedia*, there are too many signs indicating it for it to be ignored. I am not sure that *Raising Arizona* has the same interpretive levels as Dante's *Divine Comedy*, but certainly, I would say, there is more going on than just the literal story. There are too many odd parallels and peculiar events within the movie that seem to require some kind of interpretation, that seem to indicate other levels of meaning. Some quick examples are the tattoo (of Mr. Horsepower, but it also looks a lot like Woody the Woodpecker) shared by Hi and the Lone Biker of the Apocalypse, Leonard Smalls. The similar gesture of dragging someone out from under something by the foot that is committed first by Hi with one of the Arizona infants from under the crib and the gesture performed by the lone biker on Hi (dragging him out from under a car). There are weirdly unbelievable sequences like the whole pampers-stealing, gun-blasting, dog-chasing sequence or just the strangely quiescent and unharmable baby that falls, twice (!), from the top of a moving car, yet survives untouched and unperturbed.

Take for example, the polysemous character of the visit by Glen and Dot. The experience of their wayward undisciplined kids is a repetition of Hi's first experience with the unruly Arizona quintuplets when he is trying to kidnap one of them. It is a subjectivised representation of Hi's worst fear of what having a family will be like. It does not take a particular side on the nature vs. nurture question, but does definitely uphold the proverb about apples not falling far from the tree. Each of Glen's children seems to be active embodiments of Glen's concept of a joke, a thing said or done at someone else's expense that can be laughed at. Not only does one of the children squirt Hi in the crotch with his squirt gun because he thinks it is funny, they all laugh at their father's broken nose because they think it is funny. Empathy is not part of the family ethos. This is all surely also a comment on American child-rearing practices, since, I would guess, most of us have encountered such a family in the United States, but I have never seen such a one, nor would I expect to, in Europe. And we laugh at this joke, the joke that this whole sequence represents. This can be good laughter, the laughter that frees us from certain oppressions, the oppressions of families, our own and other peoples', the oppression of our guilt about feeling the oppressions of families, the oppression of anxiety about entertaining, which rarely turns out quite as badly as this experiment in entertaining turns out.

So, there are many things going on simultaneously in this sequence, and all of them tie into different narrative levels that the movie sustains throughout. All of these narrative levels, however, address the question: How does one achieve happiness? How does one create a happy home in this complex, wonderful, terrifying, maddening America? What is the answer to this question suggested by *Raising Arizona*?

The answer that this movie suggests seems to have something to do with the nature of comedy, something to do with the way seeing the comic can lead to a life lived as a comedy, that is, as ending better than it begins. This, it has to be acknowledged, would have to be the meta-narrative lesson of the movie since no one in the movie itself seems to really pick up on the comic dimension of life.

Dreams and Freedom

An important and recurring theme in *Raising Arizona* is Hi's dreams. Dreams, if Freud is right, are inherently polysemous. They have, at the very least, two levels of meaning, what Freud called the manifest and the latent levels of meaning. The manifest meaning is what we literally dream, the latent meaning is what the dream means, what an interpretation of the dream will tell us about ourselves. At least one commentator on the movie has raised the possibility that some, or all, of the movie may be a dream,[33] which would make Hi's explicit dreams, dreams within a dream. Nietzsche claims that metaphysics begins with the fact of dreams.[34] That is, with dreams we have a direct experience of a counter-narrative, an alternative reality, to that of our everyday experience. This creates a need to determine which is the true narrative or the true reality, and that question calls forth metaphysics. If Nietzsche is right, this suggests a deep connection between dreams and philosophy. The idea of a counter-narrative is what sets us free from the constraints of whatever narrative we happen to find ourselves in. This is the way in which philosophy can set us free, by empowering us to imagine other ways of being. Movies, in general, are very dream-like—oneiric is the word for that—and like dreams, seem to call for some interpretation, and, like dreams, can be a road to a new kind of freedom from what oppresses us.

"In dreams begin responsibilities," wrote Delmore Schwartz.[35] That is, in dreams we confront the pieces that are missing from the narrative that we are working with in our everyday lives. Hi's dreams are so important to the movie because the movie itself is a kind of working through the issues that are raised in his dreams. The two escaped convicts, Evelle and Gale, are like emissaries from Hi's unconscious come to remind him of his "true" nature. They emerge just as Hi is beginning to settle down into family life, and they can be seen as the part of his identity that he is not quite sure that he wants to give up yet. They are childlike, sloppy, lawless, and they live only for the moment. They are literal and figurative remnants of Hi's earlier life, when all he lived for was to be an outlaw, and when time moved in cycles so that he always knew where he was in time just by knowing where he was in a particular cycle.

At the beginning of Dante's *Commedia*, at the beginning of the first section, the "Inferno," after Dante awakes in the dark wood, he sees a distant peak with the bright light of the sun, representing goodness, shining atop it. He turns to make his way toward it, but his way is blocked by three beasts: a leopard, a lion, and a she-wolf. These beasts are, allegorically, his own sins that he is not yet quite ready to give up, things that he cannot quite convince himself are really evil. Similarly, Hi has to confront his own outlaw ways, which have been at the core of his identity. In some sense, he knows that he has to give up those ways, but in another sense, he does not know that at all and really wants to hold on to those parts of himself. That is part of the conflict within himself that Hi has to work through throughout the course of the movie. When Hi does manage to work through some of his issues, these two emissaries from his unconscious go back down into the dark hole from which they escaped. We are never completely free of those desires we once nurtured but now suppress, but we can keep them in a prison so that they never see the light of day.

The prison escape is also a kind of a joke. Their emergence from a viscous hole in the ground looks a lot like a birth. As Gale explains in Hi and Ed's living room, "We don't always smell like this, Miz McDunnough. I was just explainin' to yer better half here that when we were tunnelin' out we hit the main sewer..."[36] which is a lot like what William Butler Yeats has Crazy Jane say to the Bishop in the poem, "Crazy Jane Talks with the Bishop:" "...Love has pitched his mansion in/The place of excrement...." Life is a weird, messy business, and there is just no getting around that fact. Wisdom will have to do with coming to grips with the messiness of it, the way it does not always go the way we would want it to go.

For Hi, *something* begins in that flash of light in which he first sees Ed, but that something takes an additional turn with the remark by the prison counselor (Peter Benedek) about most people having a family that sets Hi to musing, then dreaming, then acting on an idea based on that remark. The hardest part of acting freely, if this is what freedom is, is staying true to one's original choice, remaining faithful, as Badiou says, to the event. All of the over-determining forces that would direct us along more predictable routes, including our own habits, do not suddenly vanish. On the contrary, they kick in with even more force than ever. That is what Dante is talking about when he describes the three beasts that suddenly appear just as he tries to set off on a new direction in his life. The beasts overwhelm his resolve, and it is only with the intercessionary help of Virgil that he can go on. Hi will find himself driving past convenience stores on the way home from work, and, like Dante, he will find it too difficult to resist this particular beast from his own soul.

Andrew Pulver, writing for *The Guardian* about an encounter with Joel and Ethan Coen, identifies a passage from Ethan's book of stories, *Gates of Eden,* that Pulver suggests may have some biographical relevance, but, in any event, does seem to tie in to a recurring theme in the Coen brothers' movies. In the story "I Killed Phil Shapiro," there is a summer camp director, Rabbi Sam, who says, as words of welcome to the new camp recruits, "If You Will It, It Is No Dream."[37] As Pulver mentions, this phrase occurs in *The Big Lebowski* (1998) when Walter (John Goodman) says to the Dude (Jeff Bridges), "if you will it, Dude, it is no dream."[38] This phrase captures the central metaphysical and narrative tension of *Raising Arizona*, which has to do with what is a dream and what is reality. Are the two separable—are they, somehow, intimately related?

To paraphrase Delmore Schwartz, reality begins in dreams. That is, insofar as our reality is to be really ours, a reality of our own choosing rather than what simply happens to us, then it will begin for us as an event to which we will remain faithful. The act will have consequences and those consequences will entail responsibilities. Our freedom, somewhat ironically, will depend on our being true to, and upholding, our responsibilities. This strict notion of being responsible, however, is ameliorated by the fact that these responsibilities are our responsibilities, that is, our own chosen responsibilities, rather than inauthentic responsibilities that are imposed upon us by others or by the system at large.

The Uses and Abuses of America

Raising Arizona does present a fairly piquant critique of America. The pampers-stealing, gun-blasting, dog-chasing sequence is, for me, one of the funniest pieces in the whole movie. It is so funny to me, in part, because it captures something of the wild craziness of life in America, the way that the simplest acts, like getting something from the store, can become a kind of race for one's life. It is also so funny to me because of the way it picks up a particular fear that I have about my fellow Americans and their (our) love of guns and violence and their (our) desire to shoot and destroy things. The store clerk, his mouth full of braces, has a mad gleam in his eye at the opportunity to pull out the giant pistol and start blasting away. The cops behave in the same way. Even the neighborhood dogs seem to pick up the bloodlust scent and get into the chase.

This all, also, reflects something deep in the nature of capitalism, which is at the very core of our democracy. Capitalism does foster a kind of Hobbesian war of all against all. On the surface we are all (mostly) very polite and cooperative, but there is a kind of cutthroat competitiveness that lurks just below the surface and is deeply imbued in the spirit of capitalism itself. The Arizona family reflects many of the features of capitalism. Nathan Arizona's (Trey Wilson) relentless commitment to selling himself and his furniture is a paradigm of what it takes to be successful in a capitalistic system. The irony of his oft repeated claim, "And if you can find lower prices anywhere my name ain't Nathan Arizona!"[39] is, of course, that his name ain't Nathan Arizona. Or, it wasn't before he changed it, so I guess it is Nathan Arizona, but, as it were, barely, which does put kind of a spin on his famous claim for his prices.

Nathan Arizona is an example of someone who has literally created his own identity out of his own dreams of what he wanted to be. I would say that what he wants to be seems a little shallow, and this is part of the movie's critique of America and American life, but he has been remarkably successful at achieving it. Clearly, to achieve his dream he has had to adopt a basically antagonistic stance with respect to virtually everyone around him. As he says, "My motto is do it my way or watch your butt!"[40] It is an excellent, even a necessary, motto for being a successful capitalist, although less good for making friends. Nathan's relationship with his wife seems to lack all intimacy, but we learn that there is a *little* more to Nathan Arizona than just pure capitalist.

There is a kind of fairness to capitalism and a kind of unfairness. There is a sense in which those who are willing to devote themselves to accumulation deserve what they manage to accumulate. There is also a sense that in capitalism, some have way more than they need or deserve. The balance between these two notions of fairness is difficult to parse. Certainly, Hi and Ed feel the injustice side of it and decide to act to right it. Their act is a kind of underground socialism, a redistribution of the wealth from those with a surfeit to those with a dearth. It is one of the things that political scientists remark on—that America has never had a really viable socialist movement, not, at least, in the ways Europe has. There are various speculations about why that is so. I see *Raising Arizona*, as it were, raising the question of socialism and then turning in an ambiguous answer. The movie makes the idea of kidnapping another couple's child seem almost reasonable, almost a fair redistribution of wealth, and yet, it really does not work out for anyone.

The Double Plotline or: The Good of the Bad

Dante's *Commedia*, much like Augustine's *Confessions*, can be described as having a double plotline. That is, one could diagram the narrative of these works in either of two ways. The first way would be in a kind of check shape, √, so that the first part of the narrative seems to be a descent, but then, at the crucial turning point there is a turn for the better and that would be shown as an ascending line. That is the structure of a comedy, in the classic sense. The other way of diagramming such a narrative, however, would be as simply an ascending line, /, because the subsequent ascent is completely dependent upon the prior descent. This is what Augustine means when he refers to *felix culpa*, "happy or fortunate sin." In the case of Augustine, for example, he would not have reached his spiritual enlightenment if he had not fully experienced the degradation of his sin, so his sin was a great gift, a great boon to him. Dante has to descend through hell, the

Inferno, because it is only by seeing that that he will be able to understand Heaven. So, it is not just that the good comes after the bad, but that the good is completely dependent on the experience of the bad. The bad, then, is also good.

Hi and Ed unquestionably experience a narrative descent. Their hopes for having a family are dashed. They have lost their jobs. Even their marriage seems to be in danger. And yet, they have become real people, something that neither really was at the beginning of the film. At the end of the movie they are complex enough to see how complex the pursuit of happiness is, they are complex enough to understand other peoples' pain and loss—even if those people do have a lot of babies already. To get to the way of thinking and feeling that leads Ed and Hi to return Nathan Jr. is an achievement, and one that could not have been attained without all of the difficulties of their descent. Nathan Arizona, the unregenerate huckster and *über*-capitalist, reveals a surprising tenderness toward his returned son, toward Ed and Hi, and, most surprising of all somehow, toward his wife, Florence (Lynne Dumin Kitei). It is in this tenderness that I see the authentic aspiration of America, and maybe that is not just an America thing.

The real goal is not about money or fertility so much as about achieving this tenderness toward others. It may be that such tenderness can only be achieved through suffering and loss. Nathan Arizona expresses his feelings of tenderness for his wife in terms of his fear of losing her and suggests that Hi and Ed may yet discover such tenderness for each other and that they "should sleep on it" before they do anything rash like break up their marriage. I take it that they do sleep on it, and that Hi's final dream is a dream of the tenderness made manifest in the world, specifically in Utah, the state above Arizona.

The Uberty of Liberty

There is some question about whether America really is exceptional and about the value of thinking about ourselves as exceptional. If there is something exceptional about us, it seems to me that it would have to do with the way we think of ourselves as being free, as having a right to our own opinions, as being both free to, and responsible for, developing ourselves into the self we want to be. It is quite true that, as a cynic might insist, many in America do not really have much freedom to develop themselves into anything other than what they were born to, that the idea that we are "free" in America, that this is a "free country," is a myth and a harmful one at that. Without denying that, I still want to say that there is a freedom that is not just granted but, in some sense honored, in America, and that is the freedom to dream.

"Uberty" is a (somewhat archaic) word for fruitfulness, for something that generates growth and abundance. The freedom merely to dream is, in one sense, no real freedom at all. In another sense, in this philosophical sense in which any authentic choice must begin in something like a dream, then the freedom to dream is the only kind of real liberty that there is. Ultimate happiness may depend less on how much money we accumulate and more on having a sense that our life is our own life, that we have lived a life in which we have made some choices and lived according to the consequences of those choices. To accept responsibility for the consequences of our choices and actions is what makes us fully human, and it is what makes us tender. If there is any truth in that, then the stuff of comedy, the material to make the ends of our lives better than the beginnings, may be as accessible as our dreams. The most important thing, then, is to keep dreaming, and that is precisely what Hi is doing at the end of *Raising Arizona*, making it, in my estimation, a comedy, because it is funny, but also in the classic sense that it holds out the possibility that we can make our end better than our beginning. We can laugh in welcome, like Plato's philosophers, the new recruits to the realm of tenderness for each other. As Walter says in *The Big Lebowski*: "if you will it, Dude, it is no dream."

2 | *No Country for Old Men*: The Coens' Tragic Western

The point is there aint no point.

— Cormac McCarthy, *No Country for Old Men*

Coen Irony

No Country for Old Men (2007) is, one might say, one more step in the continuing journey of Joel and Ethan Coen to say something about this country and about being a member, a citizen, of the United States of America. *No Country for Old Men* feels like a very different kind of movie from every other Coen brothers' film. It is more serious, or it is serious in a different way from their other movies. It is not unusual for the Coens to take on dark themes in their movies, but previous to *No Country for Old Men* there was always a level of what I will call meta-irony. That is, there was a level of detachment, a sense that their movies were meant to be taken as just stories, that you should not take them too seriously. To be offended by *Fargo* (1996) because it seems to be making fun of Midwesterners is to take it too seriously. Irony, however, is a tricky business. People are suspicious of the ironic because the ironic never quite mean what they say. The ironic, for their part, are more or less invulnerable to attack, since to take them seriously is to miss the point, and not to take them seriously precludes an attack. With *No Country for Old Men*, the Coens have given up their ironic detachment and made a much more straightforward movie. Certainly, there is irony within the movie, but the movie itself lacks the sheen of ironic detachment that is a part of a movie like *Fargo*.

One reason for this change may be the fact that this is the first movie that they have made based on a novel. It is not irrelevant to the tone of the movie that the novel was written by Cormac McCarthy. That the Coens chose this novel by this writer, however, also reflects an evolution in their cinematic and story-telling concerns. It is a sign of their willingness to give up some of their ironic detachment, to give up a posture of invulnerability, in order to say something more straightforward about their perceptions of how the world is. This, it seems to me, is a step into philosophy.

The previous Coen brothers' movie that has the most in common with *No Country for Old Men* is, in fact, *Fargo*. In *Fargo* there is an older, wiser police chief, Marge Gunderson (Frances McDormand) and her less experienced or savvy deputy, Lou (Bruce Bohne), just as there is in *No Country for Old Men*. In both movies, a local town police officer is confronted with some grisly murders committed by men who are not from his or her town. In both movies, greed lies behind the plots. Both movies feature a cold-blooded killer who does not seem quite human as a central character, and who the police officer seeks to apprehend. *No Country for Old Men*, therefore, is not completely new territory for the Coens, but no one in Fargo has much of a sense of irony, although the movie itself is ironic; whereas Sheriff Bell (Tommy Lee Jones), for example, certainly does have a sense of irony, while the movie *No Country for Old Men* does not feel ironic at all.

A great moment of Bell-ian irony is when Bell is reading a story from the paper to his deputy, Wendall (Garret Dillahunt), about a couple in California who were taking in older people as roomers, then killing them for their social security checks, and burying the bodies in the backyard. After Bell reads aloud from the paper, "Neighbors were alerted when a man ran from the premises wearing only a dog collar." Bell comments, sardonically, "You can't make up such a thing as that. I dare you to even try." Bell continues, appreciating the full irony of the story, "...But that's what it took, you'll notice. Get someone's attention. Diggin graves in the back yard didn't bring any." When Wendall fights back a smile, Bell says, "That's all right. I laugh myself sometimes."[41] There is a bitter sweetness in that confession that shows the deep humanity that may be part of the ironist's position. His comment, "I laugh myself sometimes" links, for me, this non-ironic movie with all of the Coen brothers's ironic movies, movies in which horrors (a Ku Klux Klan rally, a hooded kidnapped woman trying to run blindly from her killer kidnappers, the chopping off a woman's toe, for example) are treated as things to be laughed at. There is a sadness to their funniest movies and humor in their grimmest.

To Kill a Bird

O Brother, Where Art Thou (2000) is another Coen brother movie that is referenced in *No Country for Old Men*. The reference is so subtle and obscure, yet so revealing of their method, that it is worth pursuing. There is a very puzzling sequence in *No Country for Old Men* in which we see Anton Chigurh (Javier Bardem) driving at night. He comes to a bridge and there is a hawk, a bird of prey, perched on one of the railing posts of the bridge. Chigurh, inexplicably, picks up a pistol from the car seat, slows down, then, as he drives by, takes a shot at the bird. What is this about? No further reference to this scene, or explication of it, is ever given in the movie.

In the movie *Cool Hand Luke* (Stuart Rosenberg, 1967), the *über*-boss, boss Godfrey (Morgan Woodward), with an ominously theocratic name, over-sees the chain gang working the Florida state back roads is a mirror sunglasses-wearing, all but silent, figure of ominous justice. There is a scene in the film when boss Godfrey, standing in the middle of the road, raises the cane he uses over his head. One of the chain gang workers, Rabbitt (Marc Cavell), immediately runs over to the truck, grabs a rifle off a rack in the back window, then runs it over and hands it to boss Godfrey. At first you think, "That's a pretty risky move, entrusting his rifle to one of these hardened criminals," but then you see boss Godfrey take the bolt for the gun from his vest pocket. He slides the bolt home, raises the gun, and shoots a hawk flying just overhead. The scene begins with shots establishing a relationship between the chain-gang workers and boss Godfrey. One of the workers, Tattoo (Warren Finnerty), says, "Don't he ever talk?" After boss Godfrey shoots the bird, Luke (Paul Newman) replies, "I believe he just said something." I take this scene to indicate how brutally and arbitrarily violent this man can be, and that what he is saying when he shoots the bird is that he is the bird of prey to birds of prey. Just establishing the pecking order, as it were, so the members of the chain-gang can see.

This figure of the lawman who is really beyond the law, beyond, even, as Nietzsche says, good and evil altogether, is picked up by the Coen brothers in *O Brother, Where Art Thou* in the character of Sheriff Cooley (Daniel von Bargen). Sheriff Cooley wears mirror sunglasses just like boss Godfrey in *Cool Hand Luke*, with the similar cinematic effect of showing reflections of the world in the glasses, but never showing boss Godfrey's, or Sheriff Cooley's, eyes. Sheriff Cooley is as relentless in his pursuit of the escaped chain gang convict, Ulysses Everett McGill (George Clooney), as boss Godfrey is of Cool Hand Luke. Sheriff Cooley seems to be a representative of the law, but when it comes right down to it - when the law pardons Ulysses and his friends—Sheriff Cooley remains implacable in his pursuit of his own conception of justice. When Sheriff Cooley is about to string up Ulysses and his friends, even though they had been pardoned by the governor, Ulysses pleads, "It ain't the law!" To which Sheriff Cooley replies, "The law. Well the law is a human institution."[42]

Sheriff Cooley is a direct lifting from, or a direct reference to, boss Godfrey and *Cool Hand Luke*. I would not be surprised if Sheriff "Cooley" was not an intentional reference to the title of the earlier movie. Anton Chigurh's arbitrary and violent shooting of the hawk (the bird of prey to birds of prey) on the bridge connects him to boss Godfrey, directly, and to Sheriff Cooley, indirectly. To psychologize for just a moment, it seems clear that *Cool Hand Luke* made a powerful impression on the Coen brothers when they first saw it. What seems to have especially impressed them is the figure of a putative lawman that is motivated by an apparent concept of justice that has nothing human in it. This figure is not always a lawman, but has its counterpart in the Coen brothers' movies: *Fargo*, *O Brother, Where Art Thou*, and *No Country for Old Men*. There is a thin thread of allusion that connects these four films that is quite obvious once you see it, but is invisible until you see it. Until you see it, Chigurh shooting the hawk on the bridge is just mysterious. Once you see it, this scene become richly allusive and deepens in meaning.

This is why one frequently has the sense after watching a Coen brothers movie that there was more going on than one quite got. One has that sense because there is more going on than anyone ever gets. The more I see in *No Country for Old Men*, the more I am convinced that there is much more that I am not seeing. This is a very important realization to have in order to begin to really get what is going on in a Coen brothers' film. In this sense, their films are like the world: there is always more to understand; there is always more to get. The goal, then, is, in the words of Henry James, "Try to be one of the people on whom nothing is lost!"[43] That is, perhaps, an unachievable goal, in life or in art, but it is that to which we should aspire, and certainly, the Coen brothers' movies richly reward the attempt to find more in them.

Westerns and Greek Tragedies

The stories that the Coen brothers are interested in telling all seem to be very American stories. Their approach of choice is the genre film. Their favorite film genre is the very American genre, named by the French, film noir, but *No Country for Old Men* is of another classic American genre, the Western. Genre is an interesting way to try to say something about something because, as Derrida has made explicit, the "law of the law of genre" is that every new member of a genre set will deviate from and violate the apparent established principles of that genre. To return to what Derrida says about the "law of the law of genre," he says: "It is precisely a principle of contamination, a law of impurity, a parasitical economy. In the code of set theories, if I may use it at least figuratively, I would speak of a sort of participation without belonging—a taking part in without being part of, without having membership in a set."[44] This description of each new member of a genre set sounds to me a lot like what it means to be a (new) member of the set of Americans. Just as each new Coen film that has genre elements adds to and transforms the genre it participates in, so too, each new American adds to and transforms what it means to be an American.

No Country for Old Men, then, is and is not a classic Western. It takes place in the West and its main protagonists are what you might call Westerners. On the other hand, the plot revolves around a drug deal that has gone bad; it involves four-wheel-drive vehicles, semi-automatic weapons, and executives in high-rise buildings, none of which would seem to belong in a Western. There is a beautiful moment when Sheriff Ed Tom Bell and his side-kick, Deputy Wendell, are riding along, following a trail, and Deputy Wendell remarks on the tracks they are following in a way that recalls for me a moment in John Ford's great classic (and revisionist) Western, *The Searchers* (1956), when Ethan Edwards (John Wayne) and Martin Pawley (Jeffrey Hunter) are following some tracks that will be similarly fateful for everyone involved. It is an interesting connection (I won't claim it is a reference) because in *The Searchers*, Ethan says, "We'll find'em. Just as sure as the turnin' of the earth"—and they do. They find 'em, sure enough, but in an odd, somewhat inexplicable twist, there is no final confrontation between Ethan and Scar (Henry Brandon), the hated Comanche chief he has been seeking for seven years. Instead, it is Martin who kills Scar, and he appears to have done it while Scar was asleep in his teepee. Sheriff Bell is pretty dogged for a while, but he will give up the search altogether, before he finds his adversary, Anton Chigurh.

Anton Chigurh might as well be Melville's Moby Dick for all of the human compassion, or even human motivation, which can be found in him. It makes as little sense to speak of him as evil as it does to say that raw nature, a blizzard or a flood, is evil. He has principles, the equivalent in a man to the laws of nature. Given his principles, he does not act irrationally or from passion; he is more of an inexorable force. He is not a rampaging killer on the loose; he has been summoned by a human will, a human desire, to achieve a desired end. He appears only because he was summoned. The recognizable and clear evil lies with he (or those, there may be others involved, the film is not explicit on this point) who summoned him. He was summoned because of greed, lust for power, an indifference to the suffering of others, and personal gratification. He who summoned him will learn, too late, that, like the Sorcerer's Apprentice, he has summoned a power that he cannot control, that it was pure hubris to think that he could control it.

That evil man is of little interest to either Cormac McCarthy, the author of the novel, *No Country for Old Men*,[45] or to Joel and Ethan Coen, the makers of the movie. What is of interest to McCarthy and the Coens is rather what happens when a good, but flawed, man encounters this force of nature in human guise. In this sense, *No Country for Old Men* recapitulates the patterns of ancient Greek tragedy. As in ancient Greek tragedy, a good, but flawed, man will become enmeshed in events that will prove his ruin. It will be what is good in him as much as what is flawed that will engage him in these events, and his ruin will be complete. Oedipus is a kind of paradigm of the way the ancient tragedies begin and end. It is because Oedipus is so smart, self-confident, competent, and passionate that he ascends to the throne of Thebes and rules there as a good and noble king. It is also because Oedipus is so smart, self-confident, competent, and passionate that he is able to complete the mysterious task sent him by the Oracle of Delphi and to find the murderer of the previous king of Thebes, King Laius. Unfortunately, as it will turn out, it is Oedipus himself who killed the previous king, as predicted by the same Oracle of Delphi long ago. He has also married his mother and fathered his children/siblings. As a consequence, Oedipus's wife/mother commits suicide, he blinds and exiles himself, his incest-produced children will fight and be responsible for each other's deaths. Llewellyn Moss (Josh Brolin) is similarly smart, self-confident, competent, and passionate. His intelligence and competence lead him to the "last man standing" (as Moss puts it to the dying man in the truck, saying, "…there must've been one")[46] and to the money. His compassion compels him to return to the site of the drug deal gone bad to bring water to the one dying man left who asked for it. It is not at all clear whether or not Chigurh or the Mexicans would have ever picked up the transponder signals if he had not gone back, but it is certainly clear that once they have found Moss and his truck at the scene, they will be on his trail wherever he goes. A fate similar to Oedipus's disastrous ruin awaits Llewellyn Moss: both he and his young wife will be brutally murdered; all that he has will be lost.

Power, Hubris, and the Fatal Flaw

Anton Chigurh is a monster, in the sense that Emerson uses the word in his essay "The American Scholar," that is, in association with "monitory" and "admonition," drawing on its Latin derivation meaning a divine warning or an omen.[47] The ancient Greek tragedies were meant to serve that same function, that is, of warning about especially human temptations that would lead to disaster. Tragedy was considered a source of wisdom as well as of entertainment, and the primary wisdom that the ancient Greek tragedies taught was also written on the wall at the famous and perhaps most holy of Greek temples, the Oracle of Delphi: "Avoid hubris." Hubris is a difficult word to recover from the Greek, but it means something like arrogant ignorance, thinking that you are better or more powerful than you really are. The Greek gods hated hubris, and one of their primary occupations as gods was punishing humans for their hubris.

Hubris was such a problem for the Greeks not because they valued timidity or even humility, but because they loved power, and they loved powerful, proud people. As Aristotle says in the *Nicomachean Ethics*, "the man is thought to be proud who thinks himself worthy of great things, being worthy of them…." The Greek ideal was to manifest all of your true power, and to be very powerful, without overstepping your own limits, without presuming to have more power than you really have. This is a very difficult ideal to achieve because one does not know what one is capable of until one tries to do things beyond what one has done before. And yet, the Greeks (Aristotle, for one) assumed that one could know what one is capable of, and thereby avoid the calamities of hubris. The above quotation from Aristotle finishes, "…for he who does so beyond his deserts is a fool, but no virtuous man is foolish or silly."[48] This Greek ideal, this wisdom, is, too, exhorted upon the wall at Delphi: "Know thyself."

Llewellyn Moss is a man of considerable resources, but his powers have been lying more or less dormant. He has innate powers of intelligence and determination as well as some acquired abilities learned while serving in Vietnam. Virtually all of these powers are banked, the way one banks a fire, because there is no way to exercise them in his day-to-day life. He has a good job as a welder which does not require all of either his intelligence or determination. He has a lovely young wife and a comfortable trailer home, but no obvious way of improving his situation beyond this level of comfort. In many ways he seems to be happy and successful, but it is a difficult thing to have powers that you have no opportunities to use. Doing pretty well in America has never been the happiest of options if there is some chance that you could be doing better. Of course, that possibility of doing better becomes real for Llewellyn when he comes upon the briefcase full of cash. He barely seems to hesitate before he decides to go for it.

A key element of Greek tragedy is the idea of the protagonist's *hamartia*, the fatal flaw. Hamartia is a term derived from archery and, literally, means "off the mark," signifying that one's aim has been slightly off. The protagonist of a classic Greek tragedy must be essentially a good person, a person whose intentions are good, but who does not really or fully know himself or herself, and this lack of self-knowledge is mixed with a bit of hubris, which puts off one's aim. This is quite literally suggested of Llewellyn at the beginning of the movie when Llewellyn is hunting for antelope and ends up shooting an antelope in the hindquarters. In a sense, the entire movie is pre-figured in this scene. It is a scene that shows Llewellyn to be highly competent, an expert at hunting: the way he uses his boot for a barrel rest, the way he adjusts the sight for the distance of the shot, his patience in taking the shot, his picking up his shell after he takes the shot are all signs of his expertise. All are signs of his knowledge, his ability, his power, but the scene also shows his ultimate hubris, literally and figuratively. Instead of killing the antelope, he only wounds it, the worst possible outcome for a responsible hunter. He is clearly frustrated and annoyed with himself, and he heads out after the wounded antelope to try to finish what he has started.

It is a long shot that he thinks he can make. It is not a shot that he will make, but he is just good enough to actually hit the antelope at the distance of almost a mile. All of the elements of the movie are here, Llewellyn's talents as well as his misjudgments, as well as certain implacable facts of nature: distance, heat, and the movement of the antelope are the facts of nature that will undo his best intentions. His aim is good, but not quite good enough, and the worst possible consequences eventuate because he was willing to try the difficult shot. His experience is a Greek tragedy in miniature.

Our Place in the Universe

There is a problem in philosophy that is related to a problem in art and to one in science as well. The problem is, in part, epistemological, that is, it is a problem of knowledge, and it is, in part, a problem of communication. It is the problem of discovering and communicating new knowledge about the world. Take, for example, the phenomenon of gravity. Gravity is invisible. Before Newton, no one had thought of the concept of gravity to explain things as different as a falling apple and the movement of the moon. Of course, the signs of gravity were everywhere, but people did not know how to see them as signs of gravity. Then, once you have the concept of gravity, and you see that this explains the movement of the moon, the movement of the planets, and even the movement of the earth, how do you explain it to someone else so that they can understand this new and powerful concept? Well, the way Newton did it was to talk about falling apples.

A more explicitly philosophical example can be found in the writings of Heraclitus. Heraclitus of Ephesus (585-525 B.C.E) was one of the more famous of the pre-Socratic philosophers. He was known as "The Dark One" and "the Riddler" because what he had to say about human life, and the way he said it, was so pessimistic, puzzling, and elusive. He said, for example (and most famously), "One cannot step in the same river twice,"[49] which seems to be factually false, and yet strangely, provocatively true. The structure that Heraclitus developed for conveying his cryptic ideas is based on a model that Hermann Fränkel calls the "geometrical mean" which has the form A/B = B/C. Using an example from Heraclitus, he says, "Man is stamped infantile by divinity, just as the child is by man"[50] which has the form divinity/man = man/child.[51] This is a way of trying to convey some very abstract wisdom about our human position in the universe. What he is trying to convey is the very difficult, non-human knowledge that we may not be the ultimate things in the universe, that not everything in the universe is about or for us. This is hard knowledge for us to see because so much of our attention is devoted to getting what we think we want, to finding in the world the things that we need, that this becomes our primary frame of reference: the world as the source of what we need. The world, in short, appears to us to be about us. Heraclitus is trying to convey a wisdom, a knowledge, that re-contextualizes our place in the universe for us. He is trying to communicate this to us so that we might understand ourselves differently; and having this knowledge will help us to live better, more satisfyingly, in this world.

There is a similar structure in the movie, and, I think, a similar wisdom. That is, the scene shift from Anton Chigurh killing the nameless car driver with his cattle stun gun to Llewellyn Moss hunting antelope is bridged with a virtually identical piece of dialogue, first uttered by Anton to the driver of the car he has pulled over, then by Llewellyn to the antelope he has fixed his sight on: "Hold still."[52] They are the words of the hunter to his prey. The basic formula seems to be that Anton is to human beings (and to Llewellyn, in particular), as Llewellyn the hunter is to the antelope. Just as the antelope can have little or no understanding of the principles that govern and guide its hunter, Chigurh's human victims can understand about as much of what governs and guides him. It is very hard to understand people who act from motives that are very different from our own. The default position is to label such people evil or morally reprehensible, but that is more or less just a throwing up of one's hands. It is more or less a confession of being confounded. The first step toward wisdom is an acknowledgment that there may be more going on than that of which we are aware. This has always been the central goal of philosophy, to figure out what the more going on might be.

Rules and Vulnerability

Anton Chigurh is like a walking abattoir. People are just cattle to him, which makes his weapon of choice especially appropriate. He is like a modern version, one updated for a heavily meat-eating, American public, of the traditional figure of Death with his scythe. One of the most profound moments in the movie, or the moment that raises some of the most profound philosophical and, especially, ethical questions, is the moment when Chigurh asks Carson Wells (Woody Harrelson): "If the rule you follow brought you to this, of what use was the rule?"⁵³ This is the great human question, the great philosophical question. It is the question that is central to Aristotle's *Nicomachean Ethics*, where he frames it in terms of the problem of how to live a life without regret.⁵⁴ It is what lurks under Camus's claim that the only real philosophical question is the question of why one should not commit suicide.⁵⁵ That is, is there a rule that we can follow, and in following it, be brought to a place where we can affirm our whole life? Are some rules better than others? And if so, which rules, or, what ultimate rule, is the best? The desideratum is to find a rule that will free us from the fear of death, because, following it, we will feel that we lived our lives in a way that left nothing important out. Wells seems, at the penultimate moment before his death, to regret the rule that had brought him to that place. Llewellyn Moss, with increasing awareness of just where his rule has brought him, clearly has increasing anxiety about the rule he has been following. At the very end of her life, Carla Jean Moss (Kelly Macdonald) is forced to evaluate the rule she has followed that has brought her to be sitting in a bedroom across from Anton Chigurh. There is a moment when a shadow seems to pass over her face as she considers it. Even Sheriff Bell, who has some very specific ethical rules he follows,⁵⁶ and which have worked for him, seems to be undone by the end of the movie. It is as though Anton Chigurh comes as a kind of avatar of death, a remnant of the ancient Greek gods, specifically the Furies, and his function is to undo or to make irrelevant everyone's rules.

What rule, then, does Chigurh follow? There are two scenes that mirror each other and reveal something important about the rule that Chigurh follows. The first scene is the very powerful, and very creepy, one in which Chigurh gets annoyed with a friendly question from the proprietor of the gas station (Gene Jones), "Y'all getting any rain up your way?"⁵⁷ What follows is a tense exchange that subtly escalates into what is clearly a life or death situation for the proprietor. Chigurh demands that the owner call the coin toss. After some resistance he does call it, "Heads." Heads it is. Chigurh leaves the coin and walks out. The proprietor gets a reprieve. In a similar scene, with Carla Jean, although we do not see the toss, it is pretty clear that she loses the bet and is killed. (As he leaves her house, Chigurh checks his boot soles for blood, an obvious danger in his line of work.) What is interesting about these two scenes is that in them Chigurh *has* vaguely human desires. In the first of the scenes, he really wants to kill the gas station proprietor. In the second scene, one feels as though he would really prefer not to kill Carla Jean. In both instances, he subjugated his desires to the flip of a coin, to chance. That is his principle. It is the principle that keeps him from a certain kind of vulnerability. As he tells Carla Jean, in the novel, when she says to him that he does not have to kill her, "You're asking that I make myself vulnerable and that I can never do. I have only one way to live. It does not allow for special cases. A coin toss perhaps."[58] That is, he recognizes that it is precisely his feelings, his desires, which make him vulnerable. His rule—that chance must trump any desire that he might have—is in the service of maximum invulnerability. I read the sudden and violent crash that occurs right after Chigurh leaves the house where Carla Jean was staying as a sign that there are higher laws yet in the universe than Chigurh's principle. As Chigurh is to Carla Jean, so are the higher laws to Chigurh. What the nature of those higher laws is I am not sure, but Chigurh's principle is no defense against them. Since these laws are higher and counter to Chigurh's principles, there is some reason to hope that they are also more sympathetic to human wishes and desires than Chigurh is, but that is a small hope indeed.

Apollo and Dionysus: Reason and Passion

The late nineteenth and early twentieth century philosophical movement known as existentialism can be understood, in part, as a reaction against the Enlightenment period of the seventeenth and eighteenth centuries. The Enlightenment was a period of great confidence in the human ability to use reason to shed light on the ways of nature. It is not that people thought they had all the answers, but that they were convinced that all the answers would be forthcoming if methodological reason was applied to any given situation. This confidence applied to social contexts as well as to contexts of nature. The framing of the United States Constitution was an Enlightenment influenced project producing a great Enlightenment document: the United States Constitution. Science produced technology, technology created new industries, new factories and new social structures. These industries and factories and social structures often resulted in new forms of abject poverty, human degradation, and war. The philosophical response to these unforeseen, unintended, but very real consequences of the Enlightenment was to question the very basis of Enlightenment ideals. Philosophers began to consider whether there might not be some fundamentally irrational principle in the world that will always evade rational accounting. Perhaps it is the very reliance on reason—at the expense of emotion and community and art—that is the problem.

Nietzsche's first book, *The Birth of Tragedy* (1872), explicitly took on the conflict between science and art, between reason and passion. Nietzsche saw these late nineteenth century conflicts as a recapitulation of a similar conflict that occurred in fifth century Athens. According to Nietzsche's narrative, the great Greek tragedians Aeschylus and Sophocles were philosophers with a wisdom to teach, and that wisdom had to do with the importance of balancing reason and passion into a perfectly proportioned whole. Reason without passion was empty and meaningless; passion without reason was chaotic and dangerous. Nietzsche invoked two Greek gods to represent the two sides of the equation: Apollo (for reason) and Dionysus (for passion). The need to balance these two energies within us is what Nietzsche took to be the sublime wisdom conveyed in the tragedies of Aeschylus and Sophocles. Greek tragedy, however, became corrupted, according to Nietzsche, by a rather unexpected figure: Socrates. The Socratic demand, according to Nietzsche, was that everything we do be rational. When Socrates questioned people in the marketplace of Athens, his expectation was that the person he questioned should be able to give good reasons for all of his (he mostly talked with men, though there is some historical evidence that he was strongly influenced by a woman, Aspasia) beliefs. If he could not, Socrates implied that he should not believe those things. This spirit of Socratism, as Nietzsche calls it, began to infect Greek tragedy, especially in the plays of Euripides, where the sublime elevations of feeling and passion—in the plays of

Aeschylus and Sophocles—were reduced to much more ordinary, everyday sorts of scenarios that were well-explained by the chorus and ended with the ratification of some rational moral principle.[59]

For Nietzsche, dry Apollonian reason lacked all power of creativity. The Enlightenment emphasis on reason led to a kind of social sickness, a desiccated preoccupation with order and reason that made human life more or less pointless. His physicianly prescription was for a recovery of some of those lost or suppressed Dionysian energies. The Dionysian is associated with wild nature, which can be as violent as it is reproductively fruitful.

Wildness is a central tenet of our American identity. The word "wilderness" is from the Anglo-Saxon *wildëor*, a wild animal or beast, so that "wilderness" means, where the wild things are.[60] Europe, on the other hand, is associated with civilization. As Roderick Frazier Nash explains in his book, *Wilderness and the American Mind*, "The largest portion of the energy of civilization was directed at conquering wildness in nature and eliminating it in human nature."[61] That is to say, it is the progress of civilization that creates the idea of wilderness. Before there was an idea of civilization, there was no differentiation between civilization and wilderness. "Civilization severed the web of life as humans distanced themselves from the rest of nature. Behind fenced pastures, village walls, and, later, gated condominiums, it was hard to imagine other living things as brothers or nature as sacred. The remaining hunters and gatherers become 'savages.'"[62] Europeans were tamed by the social hierarchies of tradition, class, and family. To them, wilderness was something ugly. Americans, by contrast, had a wildness associated with them that came by way of the untamed land.

The history of the concept of wilderness is one primarily of opposition. The wilderness was considered a place both physically and morally perilous. The opposite of "wilderness" is "paradise," Persian for luxurious garden (nature tamed). The Bible is full of references to the wilderness as an accursed place. Adam and Eve are expelled from the garden into a desolate wilderness. Jesus experiences his trials with Satan in the wilderness. This was the attitude of the American pioneers as well. As Nash says, "The pioneers' situation and attitude prompted them to use military metaphors to discuss the coming of civilization. Countless diaries, addresses, and memorials of the frontier period represented wilderness as an 'enemy' which had to be 'conquered,' 'subdued' and 'vanquished' by a 'pioneer army'."[63] The commitment of the American pioneers was to convert wilderness into civilization, a paradise.

Where there are gains, there are also losses. This is part of the wisdom of Nietzsche, that the suppression of some part of our nature can have dire consequences to our natures as a whole. The central trope of American wildness is the Wild West. Early on, Thoreau recognized the dangers of suppressing our own wildness and of the loss of wilderness. In his essay, "Walking," he writes: "The West of which I speak is but another name for the Wild; and what I have been preparing to say is, that in Wildness is the preservation of the world."[64] I understand him to mean that, while rational Apollonian order and control are fine as far as they go, growth, creativity, real human (and non-human) thriving depend on wildness, on a principle of chaotic, raw energy. To lose our wilderness, to lose our wildness, is to lose the world and ourselves.

The Westerner, Blood, and Death

In the classic Westerns, there tends to be a divide between Easterners and Westerners. Easterners tend to be more civilized, more religious, more concerned with moral rules, more talky and much less committed to outright action. The Westerner, by contrast, tends to be closer to something wild than civilized, has—at best—a very rudimentary piety, or none at all, is concerned with a pretty straightforward conception of justice that is based on leaving him or her alone, and is suspicious of words and is committed to doing what needs to be done.[65] Llewellyn Moss is a typical Westerner in all these ways. His primary problem with Carson Wells seems to be that Carson Wells talks too much.

Peter French, in his book, *Cowboy Metaphysics: Ethics and Death in Westerns*, says, "All Westerners have something inside them that has to do with death...."[66] Jane Tompkins in her book, *West of Everything: The Inner Life of Westerns*, takes her title from a passage in Louis L'Amours *Hondo*, "...the stark features of

Lieutenant Creyton C. Davis, darling of Richmond dance floors, hero of a Washington romance, dead now in the long grass on a lonely hill, west of everything."[67] Tompkins explains, "To go west, as far west as you can go, west of everything, is to die."[68] French refers to ours as a "death-denying" culture, while the Westerner is "death-accepting."[69] Part of the power of *No Country for Old Men*, it seems to me, comes from the primal themes that it addresses head on. Llewellyn Moss is a man who is not afraid of, is not really even put off by, death. When he comes across the death scene in the desert, he does not shake or flee or weep; he is simply cautious. When he finds the last man standing (now sitting and no longer a man) and takes the money, he knows exactly what he is doing, what he is risking. Sheriff Bell, too, knows what he is doing, knows that, to do his job, he must accept the fact of the possibility of his own death. As he says, "I always knew you had to be willing to die to even do this job...."[70]

There is, in *No Country for Old Men*, plenty of death and blood. In our culture today, we are as squeamish about blood as we are in denial about death. A skinned knee on a school yard is an emergency calling for rubber gloves and immediate containment procedures. There are reasons for this to be sure. The omnipresent threat of AIDS is clearly one. For all that, however, such radical reactions to the sight of blood betoken an alienation from our own bodies and a terror of our own fluids. There is a sort of beautiful intimacy we see in the ways Llewellyn Moss attends to his own battered and bleeding body. There is a heroism, a revelation of his ferocious will, in his determination to continue to do what he intended to do, in spite of his severe and bleeding wounds. We live in a culture where our identities are largely determined by our shopping habits, where our primary concerns have to do with what car we should buy, what television or house we can afford, what demands our bourgeois job is making on us. To watch the primal struggles of a person dealing with his own bleeding body and the attention it demands to stay alive, with a killer like Anton Chigurh on his trail, promise a kind of immediate and pressing reality that is pretty elusive for most of us. We have lost something real in our loss of the experience of wildness. I am not exactly saying that I would prefer to have someone like Anton

Chigurh on my tail, or that we should be cavalier about blood spilled on school yards, but I am saying that something gets lost when we lose the risks that wildness presents to us.

Fate

A movie like John Ford's *The Man Who Shot Liberty Valance* (1962) can be thought of as an elegy for the loss of a certain kind of wildness. Tom Donophon (John Wayne) is all that a Westerner can be: a man in his prime, big, strong, and capable – as capable of tenderness as of violence. He really has no problem with the outlaw Liberty Valance (Lee Marvin), at least, not until the Easterner Ransom Stoddard (Jimmy Stewart) shows up. Ransom (with the faint suggestion of something rancid, something that is a sign of the death of something) comes to the western town of Shinbone as a lawyer and a talker, descrying lawlessness, which, for the Westerner, is basically the same thing as freedom. Tom recognizes a certain degree of truth in the things that Ransom is saying, but he also recognizes what Ransom's truths will cost that country and, especially, the men like him who inhabit it. We, the audience, recognize the same things. We cannot deny Ransom's claims for the need for law, for the need to put a stop to men like Liberty Valance, but we also feel the sadness of the loss of a man as spectacular as Tom Donophon. To be left only with people like Ransom Stoddard is a loss indeed.

Ed Tom Bell, too, is a Westerner. He is similarly clipped in his speech, preferring understatement when words are absolutely necessary. His voice-overs, however, provide a whole new range to our understanding of the Westerner. He sounds downright poetic in his thoughtfulness. This is not exactly new. It has always been an implied feature of the Westerner that he is as sensitive as anyone to beauty and morality; it is just that talking about such things could pretty well ruin them. It is not so much that Bell is revealed to be a sensitive and thoughtful man via his voice-overs; rather, it is interesting the particular form his thoughtfulness and sensitivity take. The word that comes to mind to characterize his thoughts that are given in the voice-overs is that they are philosophical: full of wonder and the attempt to put things together in the largest possible way.

There really are no Easterners in *No Country for Old Men*. They are all, basically, Westerners: tough, stoical, doers instead of talkers. There is one over-arching wisdom that seems to be shared by Llewellyn, the old man Ellis (Barry Corbin), Bell, and even Anton Chigurh. It has to do with a sort of fatalism, which is very characteristic, I might add, of Greek tragedy. This fatalism is not quite a mechanistic inevitability, but it is definitely based on the idea that you are what you do, that what you have done cannot be undone, and what decisions you have made cannot be unmade. Finally, that what you do, what you have decided, will have their natural consequences in the world, and there is no avoiding or evading those consequences. This idea is made explicitly and repeatedly in the novel, although it seems to be equally present in the movie, if somewhat more implicitly.

In the novel, there is a sequence of scenes that does not occur in the movie. Llewellyn picks up a young female hitchhiker. Llewellyn actually does more talking here than he does in the rest of the story. The woman is very young and is headed, somewhat vaguely, for California. At one point she says, "I guess I ain't sure what the point is." To which Llewellyn replies, "The point is there ain't no point." After another short exchange, Llewellyn elaborates on a point he wants to make. "It's not about knowin' where you are. It's about thinking you got there without takin' anything with you. Your notions about startin' over. Or anybody's. You don't start over. That's what it's about. Every step you take is forever. You can't make it go away. None of it."[71] Later, when Bell goes out to talk to his uncle Ellis, Ellis expresses a somewhat similar opinion about things. In response to a question, Ed Tom Bell asks Ellis about what he would have done if the convict who'd shot him had been released. He says, "I dont know. Nothin'. There wouldn't be no point to it. There ain't no point to it. Not to any of it." Ed Tom responds, "I'm kindly surprised to hear you say that." Ellis explains, "You wear out, Ed Tom. All the time you spend tryin' to get back what's been took from you there's more goin' out the door. After a while you just try and get a tourniquet on it."[72] Later, Ed Tom, in one of his ruminations, says, "I believe that whatever you do in your life it will get back to you. If you live long enough it will."[73] Anton Chigurh, explaining to Carla Jean why he, in fact, does have to kill her, says, "Every moment in your life is a choice. All followed to this. The accounting is scrupulous. The shape is drawn. No line can be erased....A person's path through the world seldom changes and even more seldom will it change abruptly. And the shape of your path was visible from the beginning."[74]

Each of these characters is expressing a two-fold understanding about the world. On the one hand, there is an inevitability, a sense that the world goes on in its way and that it does not have much to do with our human desires and concerns. On the other hand, there is a sense that we contribute to our own inevitable futures with every decision we make, with every act we do. What is perhaps hardest to live with is not the inevitability that is the result of the turning of the earth, but the inevitability that is associated with a future we are looking at that is the result of what we have done in the past. In Biblical language, we reap what we sow.

There is a difference in the attitudes of the various characters to this wisdom. Uncle Ellis seems to be past guilt or shame or worry about what this wisdom means to his life. Llewellyn, who is still a relatively young man, seems to be pre-guilt, shame, and worry with respect to it. Ed Tom appears both most hopeful, in spite of this wisdom, and most haunted by guilt and shame because of it.

Senescence: The Process of Growing Old

At one point, Ellis says to Ed Tom, " ...What you got ain't nothin' new. This country is hard on people. Hard and crazy. Got the devil in it yet folks never seem to hold it to account."[75] I take "this country" to be a reference to the particular country that they are in at the moment, west Texas; then, second, to be a more general reference to the wild West; thirdly, a reference to the United States; and, finally, to this world or even this universe, as a whole. There are several ways in which "this country" is no country for old men, although old men do inhabit it. It is a hard country, dry, hard ground, little water, not much there to keep a body alive without a lot of work. It takes the strength and resilience of youth to get on in such a landscape. That type of landscape is not just west

Texas, but the wild West in general, with its wild men, men who do not observe the social niceties and who grasp at what they want without asking, and push others out of their way. Drug dealing is simply a more modern version of the lawlessness that has always been associated with the West, especially in Hollywood movies. Lawlessness is one way of conceiving freedom, and it is a very American way. The valance of a certain kind of freedom is a certain kind of lawlessness. The more laws there are, the less freedom. Such a freedom, however, is hard on the physically less robust. The wild West is indeed no country for old men.

The United States is a wild country in a similar way, not in being lawless, but in the way its laws are designed to encourage competition. The competition fostered by the laws of the United States is mostly economic, but we love competition in almost any form. A Sunday afternoon professional football game is not for the faint of heart. As Oliver Stone in his *Wall Street* (1987) makes clear with Gordon Gecko's (Michael Douglas) paean to greed, "Greed is good!" speech, Wall Street is, itself, a kind of wild West and no country for old men.

Senescence, the process of growing old, is part of every living species, and has its evolutionary logic. August Weismann said, "I look at death as an adaptive phenomenon because an infinite duration of the individual would represent a very inopportune luxury....Worn out individuals are of no value for the species; they are even harmful since they take the place of those who are healthy."[76] François Jacob continues this line of thinking: "In every species, the most important individuals are those which can reach sexual maturity, because they are the ones with the greatest capacity for propagation. Natural selection will, therefore, adjust the optimal state of animals to the time of their sexual maturity. In humans, for instance, maximal strength and resistance to disease is reached between twenty and thirty years…Natural selection would tend to accumulate…harmful effects in the postreproductive period of the animal's life, thus favoring deterioration of the body with age. In other words, vigor in youth should in a way be paid for by senescence."[77] Evolutionarily speaking, this is no country for old men.

Llewellyn Moss visits, as it were, the country of old men in the course of the movie. When the movie begins, he is strapping strong, grown into his man strength, confident and at ease in his body. As the movie progresses, he is repeatedly shot and wounded, each hit diminishing his strength and bodily self-reliance. His bodily strength gets whittled away like Mr. Merriwhether (Martin Balsam) in Arthur Penn's *Little Big Man* (1970). By the end of the movie, much of his strength has returned, but he has had a good taste of what old age is like. And, in the end, his strength will still not be sufficient to save him.

The title of the novel, and of the movie, comes from William Butler Yeats's poem, "Sailing to Byzantium." The poem begins:

> That is no country for old men. The young
> In one another's arms, birds in the trees
> --Those dying generations—at their song,
> The Salmon-falls, the mackerel-crowded seas,
> Fish, flesh, or fowl, commend all summer long
> Whatever is begotten born, and dies.
> Caught in that sensual music all neglect
> Monuments of unageing intellect.

The theme here is certainly consistent with Jacob's evolutionary evaluation of senescence. That is, the lament that can be heard in these lines is for no longer belonging to the country of the young. It is also a lament for the way the young neglect the wisdom of the past and, presumably, of the old. The poem continues in the second stanza: "An aged man is but a paltry thing, / A tattered coat upon a stick, unless / Soul clap its hands and sing, and louder sing / For every tatter in its mortal dress...." The wisdom here seems to be that when one has outgrown the world of the young, the world aflow with sensual music, one must make one's own music, presumably, as art; for Yeats, as poetry. The poem ends with the poet imagining himself, after he has died, being made into a golden bird by some ancient artisan, "...set upon a golden bough to sing / To lords and ladies of Byzantium / Of what is past, or passing, or to come."[78]

Yeats chooses Byzantium because it was a great early Christian city in which Plato's Academy, for a time, was still allowed to function. The historical period of

Byzantium was a time of culmination that was also a time of transition. In his book of mystical writings, *A Vision*, Yeats says, "I think that in early Byzantium, maybe never before or since in recorded history, religious, aesthetic, and practical life were one, that architect and artificers...spoke to the multitude and the few alike."[79] This idea of a balance and a coherence in a society's religious, aesthetic, and practical life is Yeats's ideal, and it seems to be the very same ideal that Nietzsche extolled. It is an ideal rarely realized in this world, and maybe not even in ancient Byzantium. Certainly within the context of the movie, *No Country for Old Men*, one has the sense, especially from Bell as the chronicler of the times, that things are out of alignment, that balance and harmony are gone from the land and from the people. It is Yeats's vision, and certainly Nietzsche's as well, that it is the artist/philosopher that is most needed to help restore the balance. It may not, in the end, be the doer as much as the thinker that is needed to help us see where our losses are and where we might find the gains to make us whole.

A Dream of Fire

The movie ends with Bell telling his wife, Loretta (Tess Harper), about two dreams that he had the night before. Both dreams have his father in them. The first is about some money that Bell loses. The second has his father riding past him in the night, carrying fire in a horn. Bell ends his description of the dream by saying, "And in the dream I knew that he was goin' on ahead and that he was fixin' to make a fire somewhere out there in all that dark and all that cold, and I knew that whenever I got there he would be there. Out there up ahead."[80]

Prometheus stole fire from the gods to give to human beings in order to save them from extinction. To make a fire is an art. It is by the arts that human beings thrive, and I take that original art of making fire to stand, metonymously, for all the arts. Fire beats back the darkness, the darkness of fear, of ignorance, of hubris, of greed. I read Bell's dream of his father to be a dream of carrying on the fire of memory, the fire of the stories that one has of what one has seen in this world. It is the fire of the wisdom that those stories can yield with the telling of them. This, too, is an important role to play, to be the bearer of this fire. It is less heroic in the eyes of the world than that of the lawman or outlaw, but it is probably more important to human survival and thriving than either of those.

At the end of the movie, Bell seems to be experiencing both regret and chagrin: chagrin at how the world is turning out, regret that he could not do more to have stopped it turning out so. Ellis refers to that regret as "vanity," which it is, and, no doubt, Bell knows that too. In one sense, Bell has failed. He failed to protect Llewellyn and Carla Jean. He failed to capture Anton Chigurh. And he failed to persevere to the end. He just more or less gives up and retires from being sheriff. In another sense, however, there is great wisdom in this apparent failure. Bell knows that he is no match for Anton Chigurh. What he has done, however, is bear witness to certain events. He has seen some aspects of the world, ways in which the world unfurls, that not many have seen. It is because he was, as it were, on the front line of those events, close enough to be killed, certainly, that allows him to see what he has seen about the world. This, too, is an important role to play, to play for the sake of humanity, the one who bears witness, the one who can tell the tales of what has happened in the past, of what is passing, and of what is to come.

Section Two

Neo-Noirs

3 | The Dark Sublimity of *Chinatown*

There seems to be an almost Freudian attachment to water.

- #5 of Paul Schrader's list of film noir stylistics in his essay "Notes on Film Noir"

American film noir was always neo-noir. It was first seen as a genre, first recognized for its genuinely surprising darkness in 1946 and in France.[81] That is five years after the generally accepted year of the first instances of pure film noir, and in another country. That means that the first experiences of film noir as a genre, if it can be called a genre (as a phenomenon, if genre is too strong) already included a certain distance, a certain level of detachment, a certain re-visionary artfulness. I am not saying that the early noir films were made from this perspective, or even that, before it was identified as a genre, it was experienced from this perspective. Only that when films began to be recognized as film noir, that recognition included a detour through Europe, especially through France and Germany, a detour that did not occur when one recognized a film as a western or as a melodrama, or even as a simple detective story. This detour sets up an experience of detachment, a moment of recognition, which engages the concept of *re*-vision and *neo*-noir.

This detour also engages the concept of philosophy. The dominant post-Enlightenment philosophy of both France and Germany in the early twentieth century was existentialism, a rubric even more argued over than that of film noir. The nineteenth century continuation of the Enlightenment project looked to the future with a kind of shadow-less hope. Science, education, technological progress all seemed to promise a utopian future for human beings. The dark existentialisms of Nietzsche, Kierkegaard, Heidegger, Dostoyevski, and Sartre tracked the burgeoning recognition of the inescapable shadows that humanity casts: greed, violence, and anxiety, along with the oppression of workers, world war, crime, racial oppression, political oppression, social oppression, colonization, and then the threat of nuclear war. Existentialism was a philosophy that sought to confront the darkest aspects of the human condition. The United States in the

1940s had plenty of darkness to confront: the devastation of the Depression, world war, and the threat of nuclear destruction, to name just a few of its sources.

A central feature of philosophy is the move to abstract, to generalize, to see in a group of particulars some general pattern. This is also what is involved in identifying or discussing a genre. To talk about film noir or neo-noir is to have already begun to do philosophy. The value of philosophy is the power that is granted to those who can identify the operative patterns in a given situation. To be able to see the patterns means being able to see the opportunities that a situation offers as well as being able to see the dangers that one might want to avoid. Those that cannot see the patterns will feel like they are in the grip of fate, helpless against the forces that seem to conspire against them.

It is worth pointing out that general patterns can be extremely difficult to see. It is frequently only by some deviation in an established pattern that the pattern itself becomes visible. Why were the French able to see something that Americans could not see in their own films? The French recognized the emergent character of noir in Hollywood movies because they had not been able to see Hollywood movies for five years during World War II. When Hollywood movies became available once again in France, the French were struck by the darkness and strangeness of many of the films they were now seeing coming out of Hollywood.[82] For Americans, the continuity in the gradual darkening of certain American films occluded the pattern. The genre of film noir was doing a kind of philosophy itself. The narratives of film noir were identifying phenomena that were emerging in society at the time: new forms of anxiety, of violence, of greed, of oppression, and resistance to oppression. Neo-noir functions in a similar way, tracking emergent social patterns of its times. Neo-noir will, in addition, function as a kind of philosophy of noir. It will be a reflection on, as well as a re-creation of, the genre of noir.

So neo-noir is also something somewhat different from classic noir. It is more general, more detached, more ironic, and more philosophical than classic noir. It involves a level of self-reflexivity that classic noir lacked. To use Freudian vocabulary: classic noir tends to be obsessed with the problem of the return – the return, Freud would say, of the repressed. The past returns to haunt the protagonist or the protagonist (and antagonistic) couple. Neo-noir, at least in the movie *Chinatown* (Roman Polanski, 1974), which may be the first authentic neo-noir,[83] is more concerned with the problem of repetition. A return is still a singular event. There is the sense in a classic noir of the narrative being unique, unique both for the protagonists and for the spectators. A repetition undoes this uniqueness. The threat of the return still holds out the possibility of an evasion. A repetition, however, suggests an inevitable, an inexorable fate, an un-evadable fatality. I take the word "Chinatown" to be, in part, a sign for a repetition, the repetition of a particular tragedy, the inevitability of death in a particular kind of situation.

Chinatown, Noir, and Nostalgia

Chinatown begins, after the wistful nostalgia evoked by the opening credits and haunting music, with a black and white image of a man and a woman having outdoor clothed sex. That image is replaced by a second, similar image, then a third, and a fourth. The sequence is disorienting on several levels. There is the disjunction between the nostalgia of the opening credits and the raw, explicit sex of the photographs. The nostalgia of the opening sequence invokes a time of black and white film which seems to be reinforced by the black and white images, but then that expectation is immediately undone when the recognition occurs that these are just black and white photographs appearing in a color film. More generally, one can characterize the disjunction in terms of the intrusion of the raw into the apparent promise of the sweetly nostalgic, the intrusion of ambiguity into the apparent promise of the predictable and straightforward.[84]

"Nostalgia," the word itself, invokes the idea of a return. From the Greek *nostos* meaning "return home," nostalgia is a word for the sense that something important that one once possessed has been lost. Nostalgia is about the hope of recovery of the lost thing. Nostalgia pervades film noir because it underlies the desperation and violence that pervades film noir. It is the hidden romanticism in film noir. Wild risks are taken because of a desperate faith that the game can be won, that the lost thing can be recovered. The "thing" in the idea of *nostos* is home, or, more accurately for film noir, some romanticized idea of what would constitute a sense of finally being home. I am using "home" now as a word for feeling like you are where you belong. The idea of home is the desire for a return of something from one's childhood, when one simply *had* a home. At some point, that home that one had is lost. I take it that the desperate attempts to achieve some object, commit some crime, win some impossible love, are all attempts to achieve some sense of finally returning home, to feel like one is where one belongs. One longs for this precisely because one feels its absence. The feeling of not being where one belongs is the feeling of alienation. Alienation is the great theme of existentialism. It is a feeling that seems to have become pervasive with the rise of modernity. "Home," however, is notoriously hard to achieve in the narratives of film noir. The narratives of film noir are pretty consistently lessons on the moral "beware of what you wish for."

Venetian Blinds, Noir, and Suspicion

The photographs in the opening scenes turn out to be photos of the wife of Curly (Burt Young) taken by the private investigator he hired, Jake Gittes (Jack Nicholson), Curly's wife (Elizabeth Harding) is having sex with another man. The narrative that emerges is that Curly has hired Jake Gittes to spy on his wife to determine if she was having an affair. The photos are proof that his worst suspicions were true. He may have had suspicions, but Curly still seems to be quite surprised and upset by the fact of the matter. In evident torment, he tosses the photos against the wall, goes over to the blinds, flattens himself against the blinds, and then begins to take a bunch of them into his mouth. Jake says, "Alright, Curly. Enough's enough. You can't eat the Venetian blinds. I just had them installed on Wednesday."

It is an odd gesture, to try to eat the blinds. Part of what it means to do philosophy, to be philosophical, is to try to be sensitive and responsive to the oddness of things. It is in the odd, frequently, that will be found the signs pointing to the previously unseen patterns that obtain. It was the oddness in the post-1946 Hollywood movies that got the French thinking about a new genre that they would call "noir." Why does Curly want to eat the blinds? What does this gesture signify? Why do Roman Polanski or Robert Towne, the director and writer respectively of *Chinatown*, want Curly to eat the blinds? Blinds are a very significant visual and metaphorical trope in classic film noir. Shadows cast by light through blinds haunt many of the classic film noirs such as *The Maltese Falcon* (John Huston, 1941), *Double Indemnity* (Billy Wilder, 1944), *Detour* (Edgar G. Ulmer, 1945), *The Big Sleep* (Howard Hawks, 1946), and *Out of the Past* (Jacques Tourneur, 1947), just to name a few.[85]

For one thing, blinds—venetian blinds—are a sign, especially in the 1940's, of a certain social class, the bourgeois class, as well as of aspirations to that class. The rise of the bourgeoisie is one of the most salient features of modernity. An interesting attending philosophical development is the rise of what Paul Ricoeur will describe as the hermeneutics of suspicion.[86] A hermeneutic is just a way of looking at and interpreting some text or phenomenon. The hermeneutics of suspicion will involve looking at some of the things that are most sacred to the bourgeoisie—God, morality, love, the family, money—with suspicion, suspecting that they may not really be what they are presented as and taken to be.

The great masters of this 'hermeneutics of suspicion' are Nietzsche, Freud, and Marx.[87] There is a scene in *Chinatown* where Jake is pressing Mrs. Mulwray (Faye Dunaway) with questions while sitting at a table in a restaurant. In particular, he presses her for the name that goes with her middle initial, "C." She asks him why he wants to know. His question is one that appears to be at once banal and intrusive. Evelyn Mulwray is clearly discomfited by it, and the answer to it will turn out to be at the very center of the mystery of the plot. He says, "I'm just a snoop." Nietzsche, Freud, and Marx are *real* snoops, asking the most uncomfortable questions and discovering extremely disconcerting answers. Nietzsche will ask about God and morality. He will conclude that God is dead and that morality is just the will to power in disguise. Freud will expose our romanticized notions about love and family. Marx will raise questions about some of our deepest assumptions about justice, what constitutes social fairness, and what money is. The result of these philosophical articulations of the dark side of Western, capitalist, democratic culture is what Sartre called "bad faith" and "bad conscience." "Bad conscience" is the state one is in when one continues to act according to the norms and values of the bourgeoisie, even though one's suspicions about the validity of those norms have been awakened. "Bad faith" is a kind of refusal to see, a refusal to see that becomes a blind spot we are no longer aware of, but which haunts us with vague feelings of hypocrisy, inauthenticity, and alienation.

Visually, blinds cut and fragment an image. They suggest an inner, darker realm in contrast with an outer, brighter realm. They suggest the presence of obscurities. They hide things in the image. They darken our vision, which creates a mood of uncertainty, anxiety, and fear. The word signifies their function, "blinds." Their function is to blind, to cut off the light because we do not like too much light, cannot bear too much light. If we take "light" to be a trope for something like truth or reality, then blinds are metaphorically in the service of protecting us from too much truth, too much reality. As T. S. Eliot put it, "human kind / Cannot bear very much reality."[88] Some people, I would say, can bear more reality than others; or, at least, are willing to try to. Part of the paradox of the pain of the bourgeois reality is that it is, at least partially, self-inflicted. It is our very cooperation with the questionable bourgeois norms, our desire to use blinds, which causes our dis-ease, although what alternatives there are to cooperation, to the acceptance of some level of blindness, has always been a bit unclear.

Given this background, an interpretation of the oddness of Curly attempting to eat the blinds is that Curly wants to eat the blinds because he has had a little too much reality and he wants to recover his condition of less painful blindness. He wants to incorporate, by eating, these physical blinds in order to recover a more symbolic blindness so that his pain will be less. This is an expression of a kind of nostalgia, a desire to return to his pre-fallen home, with his pre-fallen wife there. Curly has become what, in a sense, we have all become, he has become a man who knows too much. Roman Polanski and Robert Towne want Curly to eat the blinds, not just for these reasons, but also because they want to invoke this classic image from traditional film noir. They want to announce the themes of the movie, that the movie will be about light and darkness, knowledge and the evasion of knowledge, the search for knowledge and the costs of knowledge, but with an ironic, neo-noir twist.[89]

Labyrinths, Scotomas, and Hubris

The plot of *Chinatown* is convoluted and labyrinthine.[90] The protagonist, Jake Gittes, always seems to be several steps ahead of us, the audience, but a good step behind the unfolding clues of the case. It is often confusing who Jake is working for at any given moment in the movie. He has been explicitly hired by three different people for three different cases within the context of the movie. He has been hired by the faux Mrs. Mulwray, who is really Ida Sessions (Diane Ladd), to spy on her putative husband Hollis Mulwray (Darrell Zwerling) to see if he is having an extra-marital affair. He is hired by the real Mrs. Mulwray to investigate the death of Hollis Mulwray. He is hired by Noah Cross (John Huston) to try to find the young woman, Katherine Cross (Belinda Palmer), with whom Hollis Mulwray was apparently having an affair. He also has his own interests in the case. He is invested in protecting his reputation, but he also seems to be pursuing his own line of inquiry solely for knowledge's sake, maybe even for goodness's sake.

Each case contains a counter-narrative, and so the revelation of each counter-narrative works to destabilize the larger over-arching narrative of the movie itself. The first case starts out seeming to be fairly straightforward. Jake thinks he is investigating a case of an extra-marital affair. This is very familiar terrain for him. He knows how to discover the signs that will reveal this pattern in peoples' behaviors. The down-side to this familiarity is that Jake will tend to find the signs pointing in the direction he expects, whether or not they really are pointing in that direction. Interestingly, the movie presents us, the audience, with the same seduction. There is a moment, for example, when Jake is spying from a rooftop on Hollis Mulwray with the young woman. Hollis Mulwray kisses the young woman, a moment that Jake gets on film as decisive evidence of the affair. We, too, take it to be a definitive sign that this is an affair. That is, we see it as an erotic kiss, even though, as it will turn out, it is not. The kiss itself, as kisses are, is deeply ambiguous. It could be an erotic kiss, or a paternal kiss, or just a friendly kiss, or some other type of kiss. The danger in reading signs is having a particular expectation of what the sign must mean that will occlude the real meaning of the sign. The counter-narrative is that the woman who hired Jake is not really Mrs. Mulwray, and the whole case is not really about infidelity, but about water and power, as Jake will eventually discover.

The philosopher Daniel Dennett, in discussing some peculiar features of the mind, discusses the phenomenon of the scotoma. The scotoma is the blind spot that occurs in our vision because of the way the optic nerve interrupts the field of cones and rods at the back of our eye. What is most interesting about the scotoma is that we are not aware that it is there. We 'see' no blind spot. Why is that? It is because the mind fills in the scotoma based on information, signs, from the area surrounding the scotoma. If we are looking at a tree with a pattern of leaves, the basic pattern of the leaves gets reproduced by our mind to cover the scotoma so that the visual field seems to be full and complete.[91]

There are, I want to say, conceptual as well as perceptual scotomas. There are situations in which our mind will complete the pattern according to our expectations even when the pattern is not complete, even when there may be insufficient information to complete the pattern, even when there are counter-indications to the pattern we are expecting to find. Jake Gittes is continually being confronted with the fact of his own conceptual scotomas throughout the movie *Chinatown*. He is constantly being surprised by things he failed to see, or, rather, things for which he saw the signs but failed to read them properly because of his own pre-conceived ideas about what the signs must mean. We see this in his initial investigation of Hollis Mulwray's supposed affair, especially with the photos of Hollis Mulwray and Noah Cross arguing. We see it in the situation of the "Chinaman" joke. We see it in his attitude toward the information given him by the Chinese gardener about the water. We see it in his attitude toward Evelyn Mulwray. We see it in his investigations throughout the movie until the final revelation of his final scotoma in Chinatown itself.

For all of that, however, Jake is an excellent investigator. He, better than almost anyone else, understands how appearances can be deceiving. He expects deviance, perversity, infidelity, and crime behind façades of respectability. This is precisely his problem. His expectations have so frequently been found to be justified that he has come to trust his expectations too much. He knows that he sees more than most people so he has begun to believe that he sees all that is there. What he has seen has made him pretty cynical about people's motives, but his cynicism will look naïve when it comes to the truth of the matter. His expectations circumscribe the possible patterns he will be able to see. They will create the scotoma that will prevent him from seeing, from even imagining, the real lineaments of the case. His failure of imagination will lead to the tragedy that occurs in Chinatown.

Jake's scotoma is *hubris*. Hubris, as we saw in *No Country for Old Man*, describes an unwarranted confidence, an over-arching arrogance that does not have proper respect for human ignorance, especially one's own. It is given as an admonition on the wall of the Oracle of Delphi to "Avoid hubris." It is the underlying subject of all of the great ancient Greek tragedies. The *hamartia*, the fatal flaw, of the heroic protagonists can always be framed in terms of a certain rashness, an over-confidence in their own abilities that makes them fail to respect the overwhelming ambiguities that, in fact, surround them. It is this over-confidence that leads them to their doom.

Oedipus, Greek Tragedy, and Guilt

Oedipus is an appropriate figure from ancient Greek tragedy to invoke when thinking about *Chinatown* because the parallels between the two stories are quite striking.[92] Oedipus was the first 'detective' in western literature, investigating the murder of the previous king of Thebes, Laius. Jake is investigating the death of Hollis Mulwray, the, as it were, water-king of Los Angeles.[93] *Oedipus Rex* begins with the city of Thebes experiencing a terrible plague, a situation not unlike the drought in Los Angeles at the beginning of *Chinatown*.[94] Oedipus will discover himself to be involved, unwittingly but somehow culpably, in some fairly complicated family dynamics. His culpability, his guilt, is somehow tied to the tragedy gripping his city. The resolution of the mystery of the crime he is investigating is connected to the recovery of the health of his city. Oedipus will discover that he himself is implicated in the crime he is investigating.

In many ways Jake is much more peripheral to the major events occurring in *Chinatown* than Oedipus is to the events in *Oedipus Rex*.[95] Los Angeles is not Jake's city the way Thebes is Oedipus's (since he was the king). Nor is it Jake's family that is at the center of the plot the way it most definitely is Oedipus's family. Nor is Jake a direct player in the events that have occurred. He did not kill Hollis Mulwray, nor can he save the city. Yet, given the striking parallels between the two stories, it makes sense to ask whether there is some way in which Jake is culpable, if only very tangentially, in the drought that has gripped the city. More directly, it makes sense to ask if Jake is somehow, if somewhat unknowingly, culpable in the death of Hollis Mulwray, and so is, like Oedipus, ultimately, investigating issues that go to the very core of his own identity.

The new Venetian blinds are a sign. The new Florsheim shoes are a sign, as are the tailored suits, the convertible car, the classy secretary, and well-appointed office. What are they signs of? They are signs of a counter-narrative in Jake's own consciousness; a counter-narrative to his down-to-earth, truth-searching character. Jake, clearly, has some social aspirations. To what does he aspire? He aspires, presumably, to wealth and power, to be respected, and, one might say, to leave Chinatown behind him. That is what we think wealth and power can do for us, eliminate the ambiguities and uncertainties of life.

The problem, of course, is that the ambiguities and uncertainties will not go away; they keep returning. This return takes the form for Jake, as it does for Oedipus, of the emergence of one counter-narrative after another. Every time Jake begins to think that he is getting a handle on what is really going on, another counter-narrative emerges that undoes the narrative that seemed to tie everything together, leaving him once again adrift. First, there is the narrative of the suspicious wife who wants to know about her husband's infidelity. That gives way to a narrative about the city water supply and the building of a new dam. That gives way to a narrative about money and land. That gives way to a narrative about the endlessness of the desire for power. That gives way to a narrative about a very complicated, very particular, family sexual dynamic.

That shifts the narrative to questions about good and evil, innocence and guilt, freedom and compulsion. All of these narratives seem to lead inexorably to Chinatown. Chinatown is the place where all the narratives are undone. It is the place that suggests a narrative of its own, the narrative that human beings will never figure out the narrative soon enough or completely enough to avoid the inevitability of tragedy. Jake's guilt, like Oedipus's, is tied to his refusal to acknowledge certain ambiguities in time.

This guilt is signaled in *Chinatown* with a trope that is quite similar to a motif from *Oedipus Rex*. In *Oedipus Rex*, Tiresias is the seer who is physically blind. Oedipus can physically see, but is, as it were, spiritually blind: he cannot see who he himself is or what he has done. A similar play on seeing, but most frequently via glasses, is a recurring trope in *Chinatown*. In *Chinatown*, however, the reference to flawed vision is aimed at only one eye, the left eye. Jake loses the left lens of his sunglasses at the orange ranch in the Northwest valley. Evelyn has a flaw in her left eye. Jake knocks the left taillight out on Evelyn's car so that he will be able recognize it driving at night, making the damaged car a kind of iconic sign of Evelyn herself. The eyeglasses found in the pond at the Mulwray house have a cracked left lens, and, we will learn, belong to Noah Cross. I take the fact that it is always the left eye as a reference to "sinister," from the Latin for "on the left." These are flaws in vision, signs of conceptual scotomas, which will result in terrible things happening. The one character who consistently wears glasses, but without a reference to a flawed vision in his left eye in particular, is Hollis Mulwray, the one who could see the dark events portended from the beginning. That would make him a kind of Tiresias.

Guilt, Alienation, and the Hitchcockian Blot

This is getting at the dark truth of film noir in general. Film noir worked to destabilize the overly cheerful narratives of the typical Hollywood film, as well as the overly optimistic narratives that we would construct for our own lives. They did this by showing how counter-narratives can emerge, by raising questions, in films, about our bourgeois narratives of love and family and work and money. "The bloody paths down which we drive logic into dread."[96] This is a beautiful description of the investigations of Jake Gittes, as well as of those of Oedipus. The same could be said of those of Nietzsche, Freud, and Marx. Borde and Chaumeton conclude, "All the films of this cycle [of film noir] create a similar emotional effect: *that state of tension instilled in the spectator when the psychological reference points are removed*. The aim of film noir was to create a *specific alienation*."[97]

Is the tension and alienation of neo-noir somehow different from those of classic noir? The answer, I believe, is yes. The anxieties are different because the historical consciousness is different and the philosophy of the time is different. 1974 is already well into what will be called "post" modernity.[98] It is, just barely, after the Vietnam War. It is a time when a considerable amount of anxiety was being created for people by simply an overabundance of competing, contradictory, and incommensurate narratives. Somebody had to be lying, but who and why and what would it mean for the future of our country? Philosophy was undergoing twin disruptions, one on the British/American side and another on the continental (mostly French) side. In 1967, Richard Rorty published his edited volume entitled *The Linguistic Turn*.[99] "The linguistic turn" marked a shift from the high old way of metaphysical philosophy in which the question of 'truth' was central, to a concern with language, a concern that regarded 'truth' as just another property of sentences. In France, Roland Barthes, Michel Foucault, Jacques Derrida were the new hermeneutists of suspicion, attempting a new decoding of modern values, but, like the American/Brits, paying an especially close attention to the properties of language, and the disconnection between language and the world. This disconnection undoes the possibility of any absolute truth and allows for the 'deconstruction' of any text, of any narrative. Noirs raised doubts about specific narratives. Neo-noirs, like *Chinatown*, raise doubts about getting to the bottom of any narrative.

What Jake is striving for, among other things, is to achieve a consistent narrative of what is going on. Each time a consistent narrative begins to form, signs for a counter-narrative pop up. Slavoj Žižek, a slippery, postmodern kind of thinker if ever there was one, has identified what he calls the "Hitchcockian blot."[100] It is the signifier in a scene in a movie that suggests a counter-narrative. Žižek gives as an example the scene from Hitchcock's *Foreign Correspondent* in which the protagonist, played by Joel McCrea, finds himself in the Dutch countryside surrounded by windmills. The countryside is bucolic and beautiful until he notices that one of the windmills is rotating in the wrong direction. It must be a nefarious signal system. Suddenly, all the values in the scene are transformed from quiet bucolic beauty to the sense of a dark, pervasive, presence of Nazi evil.

There are many Hitchcockian blots in *Chinatown*. Hollis Mulwray's obviously principled stand against building the new dam is a blot that Jake all but ignores in his pursuit of lurid photos of Hollis and his mistress. The photo of Noah Cross and Hollis Mulwray arguing is another one. The object in the pond at the Mulwray house that Jake notices but cannot identify is a blot. The fish in Mr. Yelburton's (John Hillerman) office and the sign of the Albacore are blots. The flaw in Evelyn's eye is, perhaps, the quintessential blot, the blot that exists for all of us. And, of course, the blinds in Jake's office are a meta-blot, not a signifier for Jake to pick up on but for us, the audience, to recognize. "Chinatown" is the blot of all blots, the blot that suggests that there is no consistent narrative other than the repetition of the undoing of every narrative.

Alienation, the Uncanny, and Freud

I associate the sense of a "specific alienation" with the experience of the uncanny. The sense of the uncanny is a sense that there is something more going on, something of which one cannot quite get a glimpse. It is the sense of the pervasive ambiguities that have not yet made themselves explicit. It emerges with the burgeoning sense of a counter-narrative to the narrative that one has been assuming obtained. Freud offers a fascinating analysis of the uncanny that provides some useful tools for unpacking the emotional power delivered by *Chinatown*.

Freud's analysis is complicated and largely linguistic, but his surprising conclusion is that, "The uncanny is in some way a species of the familiar."[101] The "species of the familiar" with which the uncanny is associated by Freud is with our infantile fears and desires. The primary fears are the fear of death and of castration. The fear of castration is, itself, a complex fear because it is a fear associated with the fulfillment of one's desire. That is, what the male infant (Freud's own blindness is reflected in his preferencing the male child over the female child) desires is the complete possession of the love object, the mother. The obstacles and prohibitions to that desire get experienced in the psyche of the infant, according to Freud, as a threat of castration. The uncanniness of Oedipus, says Freud, lies for us in the subconscious recognition of the appropriateness of his self-blinding when he discovers that he has had sex with his mother. Freud reads the destruction of the organs of his eyes as a "mitigated" substitute for the destruction of another organ, his penis. The psychological tension created by this infantile dynamic is that we desire what we fear and fear what we desire. We want what we desire and we are terrified of actually possessing the object of our desire.

Freud also analyzes the uncanniness of the *Doppelgänger*, the double, in terms of primitive and infantile fears and desires. A psychological response to the fear of death and of castration, according to Freud, is the imaginative act of doubling. As Freud says, "The double was originally an insurance against the extinction of the self, or, as [Otto] Rank puts it, 'an energetic denial of the power of death'.... The invention of such doubling as a defense against annihilation has a counterpart in the language of dreams, which is fond of expressing the idea of castration by duplicating or multiplying the genital symbol."[102]

Let us consider these ideas from Freud about the uncanny in relation to *Chinatown*. I am assuming that the movie creates in others the sense of something uncanny as it does for me. First of all, the idea of the destruction of one organ as a symbolic stand-in for castration certainly seems relevant to *Chinatown*. Jake, himself, frames the point of his ongoing investigation as an attempt to recover the health of his slashed nose. This is in the scene outside the restaurant where he has explained to Evelyn Mulwray that he was "just a snoop." His nose was slashed for, as it were, putting it where it did not belong, at least according to the ideas of some. The other prominent repetition of the genital symbol in the movie is the long-lensed cameras Jake uses to do his snooping. His strength (the intelligence that informs his snooping, the tools he uses) will also be his weakness. His considerable power to come up with the question that will reveal what is hidden will lead him to answers to questions he would rather not ask.

There are at least two *Doppelgänger* relationships that are suggested in the movie. The first is the doubling that is suggested between Jake and Hollis Mulwray. Jake seems to be Hollis's double, following him wherever he goes, lurking in the shadows as Hollis conducts his own investigations. This doubling is most strikingly suggested by the identical loss of each's left shoe, which may also serve as an additional reference to Oedipus. Oedipus's name, in Greek, means "swollen foot." This name has the literal significance of referring to a wound Oedipus received to his foot when his feet were bound when he was abandoned as an infant. The name may also have a more symbolic significance in relation to his foot, as a stand in for an organ that will be the source of some trouble for Oedipus (and, in a way, for Jake).

Although it is more ambiguous in the movie, I take it that Noah Cross serves as another kind of double for Jake. Jake's aspirations to move up in social class, his evident hunger for more money, his impassioned commitment to appear more respectable are themes emphasized throughout the movie. These aspirations are most tellingly revealed in Jake's speech. He seems most awkward when he tries to use words that he seems to associate with wealth, power, and respectability like "*métier*"; and seems most himself when he describes something moving as fast as "the wind from a duck's ass," a comment for which he apologizes, as he always does when his real self emerges through the veneer he is trying to construct.

Noah Cross, not to mention his daughter Evelyn, represents an extreme form of these very things to which Jake aspires.

Hollis Mulwray, then, would be a kind of best-self version of Jake, and Noah Cross would be a worst-self one. Jake is caught in the middle, aspiring to some kind of moral goodness and, simultaneously, to greater wealth and power. He occupies a kind of nether region between the two, desiring both and neither. Interestingly, Evelyn Mulwray is trapped in the same gray region between Hollis and her father, Noah Cross. Jake and Evelyn, no doubt, are attracted to one another because of the recognition of this shared condition, and so serve as doubles to each other. The desire each has for the other must include the desire to find in the other some way out of the terrible prison of these ambiguities. To find in the other, to find with the other, some way "home."

These ambiguities are based on mutually exclusive desires. It seems clear that it is Jake's perception that his desire for goodness can only come at the price of giving up his desire for wealth and power, and vice versa. The fear of castration that Freud emphasizes is really just the fear of a loss of one's power, a fear that will be realized if Jake achieves either desire. Evelyn loves the goodness of her husband, Hollis, and clearly, has contempt for his lack of passion. She seems genuinely, weirdly, to feel a passion for her father even as she is horrified by his evil. Can one be good and have social power? Can one find a love that is both good and passionate? These are the questions that Jake and Evelyn want answered in the positive by the other. These are questions that most of us want answered in the positive. The uncanniness of *Chinatown* derives from our more or less dim sense of these doublings, these desires and fears, these questions lurking in the background of the story of the movie as it unfolds.

Aristotle, Tragedy, and the Sublime

The first, and best, analysis of *Oedipus Rex* is by Aristotle in the *Poetics*. Aristotle's *Poetics*, it can be argued, has as its central theme the problem of the sublime. The sublime is an aesthetic category that refers to an experience that begins with the experience of fear or terror but ends in the experience of joy or awe. The central theme of the *Poetics* is explaining the power of, and our love for, dramatic tragedies. A paradox of dramatic tragedy is that which we enjoy watching as theater, as a fiction, we would be horrified by to see in real life, things like murder, death, and incest. At the theater, we do feel horror while watching these things, but we also love watching them, and feel a kind of joy and awe after watching them. This is precisely the trajectory of the experience of the sublime.[103] Aristotle intends to explain why we have this experience when we watch a dramatic tragedy.

Aristotle's explanation for this phenomenon depends on his analysis of catharsis. A catharsis is a purging, a release. Aristotle's somewhat ambiguous description of how a tragedy works is: "by means of pity and terror we experience a catharsis of such emotions."[104] The idea is that through experiencing a surfeit of fear and pity in the controlled context of a dramatic narrative we are freed of a certain amount of fear and pity that we ordinarily carry around with us, and that we experience this release with something like joy. How does an increase in fear and pity free us of fear and pity? The answer must be that there are different kinds of fear and pity. I take our ordinary fear and pity to refer to the self-preoccupied anxieties that develop in our regular lives. I take the fear and pity that we experience in a dramatic tragedy to be of a different order, of an order to get us to see, by comparison, the triviality of our daily concerns. A peek into the abyss makes having too small of an office or worry about how to afford a big screen television seem pretty trivial. To be able to see the triviality of some of our daily anxieties because one is able to see them in contrast to a larger picture, a larger narrative, I take it, is a sign of wisdom.

The Way to Wisdom

"Chinatown" is the abyss. It is the postmodern abyss of the endless repetition of narratives. We will die before we get to the bottom of the narratives because there is no bottom. That is the tragic wisdom. It is a wisdom to make us more sympathetic towards not just the futile strivings after a coherent narrative of our fellow human beings, but more understanding toward our own futile strivings for this. The tragic wisdom is the awareness of this futility. The only truth is this truth, that every truth is pregnant with the alien body of its own counter-narrative. The scotoma is structural and inherent in the fact of sight itself. This is a sad truth, but even sadness can be a basis for human companionship, for shared understanding, for the possibility of love.

Chinatown has a structure that is very similar to an ancient Greek tragedy. It begins with a man who is essentially good, but flawed, who is in a position of some power and authority, but is forced to learn the limits of his authority and power in this world, and it ends with terrible revelations and death. Several critics complained about the ending of the film, its darkness.[105] As a matter of fact, it was originally to have a happier ending, with Evelyn killing Noah Cross, and then Jake, Evelyn, and Katherine escaping to Mexico. Polanski changed the ending to the much darker one that the movie actually has. He said that the movie would have been "meaningless" with the happier ending.[106] Why meaningless? Meaning begins to emerge when we are able to begin to see counter-narratives, when we begin to be aware that there are larger narratives, narratives that put our own over-invested narrative into perspective. This is an existential narrative. It is a narrative of how "existence precedes essence," as Sartre says. Meanings emerges when we let them emerge, and not before. Nietzsche, Freud, and Marx are saying a similar thing. To begin to see a counter-narrative, to begin to see that there is more going on, larger issues at stake, is always to enter a realm of darkness, where all of one's previous guideposts will now serve only to heighten the ambiguity. Seeing more, however, is the way of wisdom, even if there is a dark side to this wisdom. It is a difficult way, not, perhaps, the way for everyone, but it is important for us all that there are some willing to take it. We can get a glimpse of that way through great art and great movies. We can get a sense of that dark wisdom, and experience some of the power of that wisdom, in the dark sublimity of *Chinatown*.

4 | Economies of Time in Spike Lee's *Clockers*

Art is more moral than moralities.

– John Dewey

The Negroes aren't the racists.

– Malcolm X

Clockers (1995) begins with signs of violence: still frames of brutally shot people, all young, all black, all apparently inner-city.[107] On the soundtrack, Marc Dorsey sings a cool jazz, "People in Search of a Life" (written by Raymond James). Capitalism is an extremely violent social system, but that violence is mostly symbolic in the bourgeois boardrooms and in the middle class experience. In the inner city, where the poverty is extreme, the violence is literal and very real. It is the dark side of the American way, of the American dream. But it is, essentially, the same system. The literal violence on the inner city streets is just the de-symbolized corollary to the symbolized violence of the system as a whole.

Very early in the movie *Clockers*, the nose of a black Chrysler Gran Fury glides its ominous way through a mostly black neighborhood of Brooklyn, New York, like a predatory shark. It represents the law, but the law in this neighborhood is not about protection so much as it is about oppression. The "Gran Fury" is on the prowl, in search of prey. Its prey are those who defy the law. The law is a function of the system and the system is, among other things, deeply racist.

American Racism

"40 Acres and a Mule," the title of Spike Lee's production company, nicely captures the deep systematic ambivalence about race in the United States. '40 acres and a mule' refers to the initial attempt by the U. S. government at reparation toward the freed slaves after the Civil War. As part of the First Freedman's Bureau Act, each freed slave would receive forty acres. The act was defeated in Congress in 1866. General Sherman ordered that '40 acres and a mule' be allocated to the freed men who marched with him. That order was rescinded by President Andrew Johnson. '40 acres and a mule', therefore, also refers to the failure of those initial gestures toward reparation. As Spike Lee says, "the name of my production company is really a reminder of a broken promise."[108] It is the reminder of a broken promise by the U. S. government, and a reference to the perpetuation of systematic racism in the U. S.

'White'[109] Americans hate racism and embrace racism, the former overtly, the latter covertly, but both sincerely. If the "Gran Fury" signifies an element in the great system of American racism, racism in so concentrated a form that it has become a physical object, and if that object also signifies the system as a whole, a kind of microcosm of the macrocosm, then why the *fury*? The fury that that car seems to represent would be the fury of white people toward black people, but why, in a racist society that favors white people, would white people feel such fury toward black people?

Since the fury cannot be based on the sense of systemic injustice the white people experience, it must be based on some fear. The fear, presumably, is of the loss of something. It is the result of a sense of vulnerability, a fear, perhaps, that the system itself, a system upon which they feel dependent, may fall apart. It is the fear, I would say, of losing their status as 'white'. In any event, the fury that this fear gives rise to is a fury to maintain the system, expressed through the laws enacted by a largely white federal government and judicial system, and enforced by the police forces of our cities, which may not be mostly white at all.

There are two ways of understanding racism. There is personal, individual racism, which anyone can manifest. Then there is systemic racism, the racism inherent in the U. S. cultural and economic system as a whole, so that all white people receive some advantage within the system for being white, and all black people receive some disadvantage for being black. In this latter way of understanding racism, it is appropriate to say that all white people are racist and no person of color can be a racist. As it was phrased by the National Education Association: "In the United States at present, only whites can be racists, since whites dominate and control the institutions that create and enforce American cultural norms and values…blacks and other Third World peoples do not have access to the power to enforce any prejudices they may have, so they cannot, by definition, be racists."[110] This was written in 1973, and even though we have a 'black' president, insofar as 'white' people continue to "dominate and control the institutions that create and enforce American cultural norms and values," it is still true today. What this means is that the system, the education system, the police system, the system of government, the economic system, will all look radically different depending on whether you are a person of color (disadvantaged by the system) or a 'white' person (advantaged by the system). This is an insidious double-ness of the American system as a whole.

Ironies of Time

"Clockers" are the drug dealers on the streets, selling drugs 24/7, hence always on the clock. The ironies are legion. "On the clock" is the expression of hard-working Americans for being at work. The clockers are also hard-working Americans at work, except there is no time clock they clock into, and they work outside the legal system. It is as though they accept the values of the larger (legal) social system, but that system does not accept them, so they feel compelled to work outside the system. What they sell is a form of relief from the oppression of the system. A way of describing this relief is in terms of time. The system enforces a strict notion of chronological time, time by the clock, *kronos* time. Drugs provide a release from that kind of time into something like what the ancient Greeks thought of as 'heroic time,' or *kairos* time.

The movie opens with temporal jump cuts of Strike (Mekhi Phifer), the central protagonist of the movie. Strike surveys the scene. He appears to be a very alert, healthy young man. What we will learn is that he suffers terribly from what appear to be ulcers. Ulcers are supposed to be the affliction of white middle-management men, men with a lot of responsibility and very little power; men so taxed by this combination of responsibility and powerlessness that their bodies take on the stress; their worry and frustration become internalized and their bodies attack themselves, causing the ulcers. This combination of responsibility and powerlessness is not, of course, the sole prerogative of middle-management white men. It is clearly exactly the situation in which Strike finds himself, and he is suffering horribly from it.

The plot of *Clockers* involves two brothers, a murder, and a cop intent on solving the murder and bringing the murderer to justice. Strike seems to be the bad brother. Victor (Isaiah Washington) seems to be the good brother. Rocco Klein (Harvey Keitel) seems to be a racist cop, although his persistence in pursuing justice rather than an easy arrest complicates his character. The murder occurs at a fast food, fried seafood restaurant called Ahab's, complete with a neon white whale on top of the restaurant and a black whale with a saddle for children to ride on by the front door. There does not seem to be an actual fast-food seafood chain by this name, so I take it that this is Lee weighing in on the great subject of Melville studies: the symbolism of the white whale Moby Dick. I read the white whale as, ironically enough, a symbol of the legacy of racism in the U. S. The neon sign of the whale on top of the restaurant has several pink harpoons stuck in its side. As a nation, we have taken some shots at this specter of evil lurking under the surface of so much of American life, but we certainly have not killed it.

There are various strands to the plot of the movie. The central strand is Rocco's conviction that it was Strike and not Victor who shot Darrell Adams (Steve White) outside the Ahab's restaurant, even though Victor has confessed to the killing. Rocco is convinced that Strike is the killer, that Victor is trying to cover for his brother, and he, Rocco, is trying to pressure Strike into confessing. One way he tries to do this is by arresting Strike's street boss, the older local drug-pin Rodney (Delroy Lindo), and making Rodney think that it was Strike who set him up. The general idea seems to be that either Rodney will kill Strike, which would be one kind of justice, or, Strike will have to go to the police for protection, and that would mean confessing to the shooting, which would be another kind of justice.

A subplot of the movie has to do with the friendship between Strike and a young boy, Tyrone (Pee Wee Love). The scenes between Strike and Tyrone reveal how caught Strike himself is between childhood and the ugly realities of adulthood. They also reveal how easily the sins of the adults get passed on to the next generation, even when the adults are well-meaning, as Strike seems to be toward Tyrone. Tyrone's mother, Iris (Regina Taylor), is ferociously protective of her young son, but to little avail. Strike's own mother, it is suggested, fought a similar battle to protect her sons, but lost it in the case of Strike. In a way, she lost it with Victor as well, although she may have the power to redeem Strike, or even both of her sons, in the end.

Similarly, Iris represents an option of redemption to Strike. There is a certain erotic tension in Iris's fury at Strike. Iris is not much, if any, older than Strike, and each may be precisely what the other needs. Strike needs a commitment to something real, as opposed to his unreal, and unrealistic, commitment to selling drugs and making money. Iris, I won't say 'needs', but would probably like a partner, a father for her son, and a companion who is her equal in intelligence, compassion, and even idealism. Strike, in his way, or, at least, in his potential, is all of those things. Both Strike and Iris could probably really use, and would probably really enjoy, an erotic embrace and skirmish. That there is not even the slightest gesture toward this possible development is further testimony to the extreme duress imposed by the circumstances that they are living under.

Gift Economies versus Commodity Economies

Lewis Hyde, in his book, *The Gift: The Erotic Life of Property*, contrasts two very different kinds of economic systems: gift economies and commodity economies. Gift economies work by means of the circulation of gifts. Commodity economies work by the circulation of capital (money) and commodities (things that have a price). Both economies produce a surplus, a kind of remainder that results from the act of exchange. In the gift economy, the surplus is human relationship, which entails certain social responsibilities. In commodity economies, the surplus is called 'profit,' and it is a surplus of extra money that is generated by the exchange.[111] Profits can be saved up in a way that the surplus from gift exchanges cannot: in a bank.

Tribal societies tend to be based on gift economies. Hyde specifically talks about gift economies among, for example, the North Pacific tribes of the potlatch like the Kwakiutl, the Tlingit, and the Haida,[112] but Native Americans now living on a reservations also (mostly) function according to gift economies. The official system of most industrialized western countries, like the United States, functions according to the commodity economy known as 'capitalism.' In commodity economies, everything is capable of acquiring a price. The central working principle of capitalism is that the acquisition of profit is a good thing. Gift economies can work within commodity economies, as little eddies of counter-narratives to the larger official narrative of the official system, which is capitalism. Churches, social groups, family groups all tend to operate more according to the logic of the gift economy than to that of the commodity economy. Various forms of gifts are exchanged, and various forms of social responsibility are formed as a result of those exchanges. Commodity economies exist, for the most part, in accordance with the logic of chronological time. Gift economies exist, for the most part, in accordance with the logic of kairotic time; they are more responsive to the movement of the sun and moon than to clocks and calendars. In commodity economies, clocks are essential. In gift economies, there is no real need for clocks. Gift exchanges work in temporal patterns more attuned to the rhythms of hours, days, months, and years, rather than in seconds or minutes.

Double Consciousness

Two kinds of economies, two forms of time, two forms of racism, two systems of values—the reality of these dualities are precisely captured in W. B. Du Bois's description of a "double consciousness" in his important book, *The Souls of Black Folk*:

> It is a peculiar sensation, this double-consciousness, this sense of always looking at one's self through the eyes of others, of measuring one's soul by the tape of a world that looks on in amused contempt and pity. One ever feels his twoness—an American, a Negro; two souls, two thoughts, two unreconciled strivings; two warring ideals in one dark body, whose dogged strength alone keeps it from being torn asunder.[113]

Du Bois is talking about the experience of African Americans here, but it is so poignant a description, and so powerful a concept, this idea of a "double-consciousness," precisely because it is something everyone experiences to some degree.[114] It is a feature of our "thrownness," to use a phrase from Martin Heidegger, the fact that we find ourselves thrown into a world we did not chose, saddled with a gender, an ethnicity, a nationality, a socio-economic status, a family, none of which we have chosen, and none of which we can fully escape.

There are two sequences of scenes early in the movie that well capture this idea of double-consciousness, which I am interpreting as being about inhabiting a space in which the dualities of commodity economy and gift economy, chronological time and kairotic time, individual racism and systemic racism, and a system of values oriented around human relations versus a system of values oriented around money simultaneously obtain. The first scene is one in which the clockers are, in a phrase used by Zora Neale Hurston, "playin' de dozens."[115] That is, they are engaged in a kind of competitive verbal play on the subject of whether a hip hop artist can be authentic if he doesn't do what he raps about. They are arguing about the hip hop group Public Enemy and their front man Chuck D, who "ain't shot nobody." The scene is about pure gift economy, kairotic time, and oriented around establishing social relationships. As they talk, they move around, physically enacting the realignments in social relationship as they develop through the game. From the commodity economy perspective, this activity is a waste of time, and since time is money in this economy, it is also a waste of money, which means a total perversion of the appropriate sense of values. It is Strike, he of the tormenting ulcers, who enforces the return to the other consciousness, the consciousness of the commodity economy of market values. He says, "We got to be about business."

What follows that sequence of scenes is a sequence of scenes in which a drug deal goes down. The drug deal is amazing. The whole process is like a military operation: complexly organized, well-disciplined, and precisely executed. What is bitterly amusing in this scene is how orthodoxly capitalistic it is. What they are doing is illegal, sure, but the way they are doing it conforms to what Jean-François

Lyotard calls "the logic of maximum performance,"[116] the logic of efficiency, which is the central principle of a capitalistic economy. What they are doing is not fighting the system so much as imitating it and recreating it as accurately as they are able, but outside the official system itself.

This homage to the system, this reproduction of the system, means nothing to the system itself, or rather, it is seen as a threat to the system since, among other things, it puts capital into the hands of those who should not have capital. In the film, representatives of the official system immediately descend upon this mini-capitalist system to crush it. All of those complicated maneuvers of evasion are, ultimately, pointless. The police can shake the whole lot of them down at any time and they do.

This situation is even more complicated than it first appears. Slavoj Žižek identifies what he calls the "politics of drugs." He asks the question, "Was it really an accident that, at the very moment that a strong self-organized collective of those outside the law emerged, it was soon corrupted by hard drugs—from African American ghettos after the rebellions in the 1960s and Italian cities after the workers' unrests of the 1970s up to today's *favelas*?" The answer that Žižek gives to his own question is, "Those in power knew full well when to use drugs as a weapon against self-organized resistance."[117] This answer is anticipated in the "Action Manual" of the National Education Association: "What white Americans have never fully understood…is that white society is deeply implicated in the ghetto. White institutions created it, white institutions maintain it, and white society condones it."[118] The logic of why is obvious enough: the ghettos maintain a social structure that favors 'white' dominance. The logic of how is more complicated and obscure, but is reflected in the way Lee has represented the relationship between the police and the clockers. Their relationship is characterized sometimes by tolerance, sometimes by arbitrary raids, and sometimes by covert and illegal bribery or coercion. It is out of this complicated mix that the social institutions 'manage' and control the status quo of the ghettos.

The Ethics of Anguish

The next scene sequence makes explicit the reality of Du Bois's concept of 'double-consciousness'. There is a police raid. The police are shaking down the clockers, looking for drugs, looking for cash, looking just to harass the drug dealers. They are especially thorough in their examination of Strike, insisting on examining his various private body parts. The scene recreates an examination at a slave sale, in which a human being, a slave, is examined thoroughly to determine his or her worth – the mouth is examined, the haunches slapped, etc.[119] The pretense is looking for hidden drugs, but the indignity, the disrespect, the values reflected indicate that Strike is the equivalent of an object, to be examined like any other object.

This humiliating, intrusive examination is simultaneously juxtaposed and intercut with shots in slow motion, which seem to indicate different time-worlds. The juxtaposition is between Strike looking from, and dealing with, the police, to him looking over his shoulder and up at a window in the tenement building behind him at his mother. His mother is grimly watching it all happen, watching the humiliation and oppression of her son. This scene enacts and makes manifest Du Bois's concept of 'double-consciousness' that people of color are forced to maintain. Our identification with Strike, however, complicates this simple interpretation. The way the scene is shot from both the perspective of an observer of the shake-down and from the point of view of Strike himself leads us as the audience, everyone, white and black, to actually experience this sense of double-consciousness. Not everyone can see the workings of systemic racism, but everyone has a mother and can feel, from the inside, the poignancy of a mother having to watch the degradation of her son and of a son having to be humiliated in front of his mother. This, it seems to me, is Spike Lee's ultimate goal. It is not so much to simply show the ways in which systemic racism is still going on. It is not to make us think that racism is bad. It is to get us to feel the anguish that these people feel. It is to make us feel like what we are watching is a human drama, a drama that we all have an investment in because, in some sense, it could be about any of us. We all share, I think, in Du Bois's 'double-consciousness' to some degree. It is precisely for that reason that we can empathize with the characters in Spike Lee's movie. Once one can see and feel their anguish, and see how their anguish is caused by elements of an unfair system, a system that we had not previously seen as unfair in this way, then what Spike Lee is doing becomes not just ethical, but political. Dan Flory puts Spike Lee's achievement into a larger context of the development of black political filmmaking. He says, "Black film's artistic development illustrates more generally how *film noir*, by virtue of its capacity to urge audiences to question the validity of assumptions that guide their moral judgments, may function to criticize the unfairness of existing social orders."[120]

Music, Irony, and Philosophy

The point of view shots from Strike's perspective get us into the movie. The cool jazz score accompanying the scenes of real violence that begins the movie, and recurs throughout the movie, lets us step out of the movie. The musical score allows us to detach from the violence, the humiliations, and the tensions of the movie, to think about what we are seeing. It is essential for our appreciation of a tragedy, according to Aristotle, that we know it is a fiction, that we know it is only a play. If we think what we are seeing is really happening, we would be horrified. We need a certain amount of detachment to receive the moral lesson that tragedies have to teach. We need some detachment to do the *philosophical* work of understanding what we are seeing and experiencing.

It is Richard Rorty's project in *Contingency, Irony, and Solidarity* to make clear what the pragmatic project is with respect to certain forms of social injustice. Rorty accepts that human beings are essentially tribal, hence very prone to racism, exclusionary behaviors, insider-outsider thinking. However he thinks the solution to these, perhaps, genetically instilled dispositions, is simply to re-narrativize who is on the inside, who is part of the group. As Rorty puts it, the project is "a shared, social effort—the effort to make our institutions and practices more just and less cruel."[121] This, as a matter of fact, is precisely what has happened in the melting pot of America. The concept of being 'white' is a social construct. It is a narrative of who is what. It is a narrative that can be re-narrativized. In the book *White Privilege*, for example, there are essays all about which ethnic groups living in the United States had their status changed from that of non-white dangerous minority to 'white.' Italian immigrants were not 'white' and then they became 'white'. The Irish immigrants also became 'white.' Eastern European immigrants became 'white.' Jews became 'white.' Outsiders become 'white' when the system stops identifying them as Other and starts accepting them as members of the system.[122] This is not done individually, but emerges as a kind of consensus. What is necessary for this consensus to emerge is some kind of narrative that makes the experience of 'those' people seem familiar to people like 'us.' This is the project in which I see Lee engaged.

The Sorites of Love

There is a sorites paradox at the core of racism: how many racist thoughts does a person have to have to be a real racist? I would say, having one racist thought inadvertently pass through your head does not make you a racist. Do two racist thoughts? Do three? There does not seem to be a set number, but at some point, if the person is having racist thoughts all of the time, you want to say, well, he's a racist. Most of 'white' Americans, it seems to me, live in the penumbra, the area of maximum ambiguity. They have too many racist thoughts to be totally innocent on the issue of racism, but their intentions and commitments are decidedly anti-racist, and so they are stuck in a sorites paradox. It is hard to say precisely what term applies to them.

The great American philosopher, one of the original pragmatists, Charles Sanders Peirce described what I will call a sorites of love. He developed the paradox by preaching what he called a counter-gospel, the gospel of hate. In his essay "Evolutionary Love," Peirce says, "self-love is no love" and adduces a quotation from Henry James, Sr., that Peirce claims effectively solves the theological problem of evil: "It is no doubt very tolerable finite or creaturely love to love one's own in another, to love another for his conformity to one's self: but nothing can be in more flagrant contrast with the creative Love, all whose tenderness *ex vi termini* ['from the force of the term'] must be reserved only for what intrinsically is most bitterly hostile and negative to itself."[123]

The sorites of love is that there is a continuum between love and hate. In some sense, according to this conception of authentic love, there can be no real love without hate. Love without hate is just self-love, which is no love at all. 'Hate,' here, just means an encounter with an *other*, an encounter with something or someone in whom one can find no traces, or few traces, of oneself. To transform the sense of repellence we feel toward such otherness into affection, connection, and affirmation, which is to say, real love, will take a new way of seeing the other, a new perspective, a new narrative of what 'they' are doing, and of what 'we' are doing. That is the work that Spike Lee is doing in *Clockers*. He is working with peoples' perspectives, attempting to re-narrativize what we see, to transform peoples' hate and fear into love and compassion.

There is a scene in *Clockers* in which Rocco is interviewing Victor in an interview room at the police station. The walls are bare and the room is dark except for a bright interrogation light. There is a darkened mirror on the back wall. Rocco is convinced that Victor is lying to him, or, at least, hiding something from him. Specifically, Rocco is convinced that Victor did not do the shooting that he has admitted to and that he is covering up for his brother Strike. Rocco is convinced of this because of his own self-trust (his own self-love). He believes he can tell a "bad one" from a "good one" and that Victor is one of the "good ones" and Strike is most assuredly one of the "bad ones." There is a beautiful, subtle, powerful moment in this interrogation in which the camera focuses on an image on the surface of Victor's right eyeball: it is the reflection of Rocco in Victor's eye. It is an amazing shot. I understand what we are seeing to be an image of what Rocco is seeing, namely, his own reflection.[124] When Rocco looks into Victor's eyes, Rocco does not see Victor, does not see into Victor's soul, what Rocco sees is Rocco. What Rocco sees, in other words, is precisely, and only, what Rocco wants to see, what Rocco is looking for, what Rocco *knows* is there. This is self-love (which is not really love) expressed as racism.

What would Rocco see if Rocco could see into Victor's soul? If he could really see Victor at all, he would see how "tired" Victor was. "Tired" is Victor's own self-description. He says several times, "I was just so tired." The very word used by Rosa Parks for why she would not rise from her seat on the bus on December 1, 1955, in Montgomery, Alabama.[125] What he is tired of is the oppression of the "double consciousness" he is forced to live with and maintain day in and day out. He is tired of having to restrain his feelings of anger and frustration that that double consciousness demands. He is a smart, competent, black, inner-city man trying to play by the rules of the system, and it is wearing him down. One thing that the system is very afraid of, one thing that the system will not tolerate, is anger from such men... yet the anger is justified. In the essay by Cornell West, "Malcolm X and Black Rage," West says of Malcolm X:

> The substance of what he said highlighted the chronic refusal of most Americans to acknowledge the sheer absurdity that confronts human beings of African descent in this country—the incessant assaults on black intelligence, beauty, character, and possibility. His profound commitment to affirm black humanity at any cost and his tremendous courage to accent the hypocrisy of American society made Malcolm X the prophet of black rage....[126]

Our "Intuitions" versus Our "Deepest Moral Commitments"

In the book *Living High & Letting Die: The Illusion of Our Innocence*, Peter Unger distinguishes between what he calls our "intuitions" and our "deepest moral commitments."[127] This is just another form of double-consciousness. Our 'intuitions' are the habits of judgment with which we have been inculcated by the system. They are judgments that serve the system, and if you are of the group that is privileged by the system, they are the judgments that are also self-serving. They seem to be moral judgments, but they are really ideological judgments. 'Our deepest moral values', on the other hand, are just that—our real, authentic, deepest moral values. People's 'intuitions,' if they are 'white,' will tend to be racist, whereas their 'deepest moral judgments' will be horrified by racism. Our 'intuitions' will constantly present us with rationalizations for the 'justice' of our racist beliefs, votes, and actions. It will take a very specific confrontation with the humanity of the people that our racist 'intuitions' concern in order to bring forth our 'deepest moral judgments.'

Our intuitions say, "Those clockers should stop clocking and get *real* jobs." Victor is Spike Lee's answer to those moral intuitions. His situation engages our deepest moral commitments. We can see and feel the soul-deadening sacrifices he makes in order to try to work within the system as it is. We can see how just getting a legitimate job does not necessarily, or even possibly, make the system work for you. We can see his anguish.

This conflict between one's 'intuitions' and one's 'deepest moral commitments' is precisely the experience that Rocco has by the end of the movie. He has been directly confronted with the fallaciousness of his 'intuitions' about Strike and Victor. He has become aware of the immense complexities of both of these men, and of their anguish. In a sense, if more indirectly, he has been confronted with the anguish of all the people he has been dealing with connected to the two men: their mother, Victor's wife, the drug lord Rodney, little Tyrone, everyone. In the last scene of the movie, Strike asks Rocco why he pursued the case for as long and as far as he did. Rocco gives him no answer, but one of Louis Farrakan's Nation of Islam workers selling the Farrakan paper, *The Final Call*, brings a copy of the paper up to Rocco's car window. The headline reads, "Justice in Black and White." Rocco just nods his head. It was not the justice he thought he wanted, but it is justice sure enough.

Hate K.O.'d by Love: The Way Out of the Double Consciousness

Peirce says, "The movement of love is circular, at one and the same impulse projecting creations into independency and drawing them into harmony."[128] This movement of what Peirce calls 'love' is meant to apply to the way that evolution works in the world as well as to the way that evolution works in society and in human relationships. The idea is that the way to understand the world is as in a constant process of evolution, and evolution is a process of forming new creations and simultaneously establishing some kind of harmony among the things that already exist.

This evolutionary process has its own logic which is, according to Peirce, the logic of Firstness, Secondness, and Thirdness. In terms of human experience: Firstness is the experience of being in a kind of bubble of unawareness. This is pure self-love (which is non-love). It is the condition of the unreflective racist. It is the condition that our 'white' social institutions want to maintain in us. Secondness is the state of sudden awareness. It is experienced when one becomes aware of an element that does not fit our assumptions, does not fit into our working narratives. It is the experience of pure Otherness. Thirdness is achieved when we see how this Otherness can be re-narrativized into a consistent whole. It is when we move beyond the narrative we have been using, which has no place for this new element, and recognize a new narrative in which this new element has a place, function, and purpose that we can understand. Thirdness is the way out of the doubleness of the "double consciousness" that du Bois identified.

This is an understanding of the way the world works that Spike Lee, as a good American pragmatist, as an inheritor of the wisdom of the American pragmatists, well appreciates. It is stated as explicitly and comprehensively as it could be in any philosophical text in the speech by Radio Raheem (Bill Nunn) to Mookie (Spike Lee) in Spike Lee's *Do the Right Thing* (1989):

> Let me tell you the story of "Right Hand, Left Hand." It's a tale of good and evil. Hate: It was with this hand that Cain iced his brother. Love: These five fingers, they go straight to the soul of man. The right hand: the hand of love. The story of life is this: Static. One hand is always fighting the other hand; and the left hand is kicking much ass. I mean, it looks like the right hand, Love, is finished. But, hold on, stop the presses, the right hand is coming back. Yeah, he got the left hand on the ropes, now, that's right. Ooh, it's the devastating right and Hate is hurt, he's down. Left-Hand Hate K.O.ed by Love.

"...Hate K.O.ed by Love" is Peirce's whole philosophy of evolutionary love summed up in a phrase. It describes the way art works, the way art narrativizes the struggles of Love and Hate, conflict and over-coming, with Love triumphing, if only in the work of art itself, which holds the various strands of the narrative together. This is Love as a Peircean Third, the way of re-narrativization, of interpretation and mediation. The mediation itself, is full of tensions, which are themselves potentially generative: of new meanings, new interpretations, new understandings, and even of new artworks.

Dewey, a student of Peirce's, says, "Art is more moral than moralities."[129] I understand him to mean by this that art manifests this evolutionary process of self-overcoming that dogmatic moralities, more or less, deny. In so far as moralities are about moral rules and judgments, they are fixed, dogmatic, and inflexible. In so far as moral improvement is possible, it will take an understanding that is open, responsive, and flexible. This kind of art, then, becomes an opportunity, first, for individual self-critique (hence of self-overcoming), which in turn becomes an opportunity for social critique (critique of the society that created the self that needs over-coming). These processes of over-coming are driven by a desire for something better, a 'love' for a better self and a better society, and are versions of what Peirce calls "evolutionary love." This is the most moral activity of all, and art is its primary source.

This spirit of evolutionary love, this idea of the on-going struggle between Love and Hate, with the ultimate triumph of Love is well captured by the word Darwin used to describe the way evolution works, "adaptation." 'Adaptation' refers to the creation of new species, and to the process of various species changing to fit together within a given ecosystem. We do this in our interpersonal lives, we change and we change those who we live with in ways that make it possible to live together. This is precisely the process that Peirce calls "evolutionary love." This is the process that Spike Lee is devoted to in the creation of his movies. It's the process that most specifically underlies the film *Clockers*.

5 | Art, Sex, and Time in Scorsese's *After Hours*

Sex and art are the same thing.

— Picasso

After Hours (1985) was an important film for Scorsese. He had completed *The King of Comedy* in 1983 and it was a commercial flop. He then made his first attempt at what had long been a dream film of his to make, *The Last Temptation of Christ,* from the novel by Nikos Kazantzakis, *The Last Temptation*, but when the filming spiraled over budget and a major theater line said that they would not show the film, the producers withdrew all funding and filming had to be abandoned. People, the money people, were losing confidence in Scorsese and he was losing confidence in himself. He needed an inexpensive, successful movie to regain the lost ground. He made *After Hours* and won the Best Director award at the Cannes Film Festival for it in 1986.

Opening Sequence

After Hours begins in an open office area full of desks topped with computers, phones, papers, and general office clutter. We hear the click of typewriters, the hum of computers, and see people moving around busy at their work. The camera tracks its way through this busy space until it comes to rest on the scene of two men, Paul Hackett (Griffin Dunne) and Lloyd (Bronson Pinchot, the character is not given a last name), sitting before a computer. Paul is teaching Lloyd, who is obviously a new recruit to the office, some things about computer programming. When they get through the particular maneuver they are working on, Lloyd confesses to Paul that he does not really care about this work, that for him it is only temporary, and that his real interest is in literature and starting his own publishing house. As soon as Lloyd starts his confession, Paul seems to be sent into a kind of fugue state that is marked by the non-diegetic music of Bach's "Air Overture Nr. 3 in D." In this fugue state Paul's gaze moves apparently randomly around the office space, alighting upon particular details that do not seem to have any connecting meaning or pattern: a phone, a person's fingers typing on an electric typewriter, a calendar, a photo of someone's child. The mention of art, by Lloyd, seems to send Paul into a kind of interstitial space and time, a kind of secret realm of mind within the regimented space-time of the office, a realm that has always been available to Paul, but one senses, not often accessed by him. This realm is dominated by a counter-logic to the institutional logic of the office space, and it seems to be a primarily aesthetic logic. His fugued gaze isolates particular tableaus of objects for no particular purpose other than the beauty of their compositions. This fugue state, if the music is to be believed, continues even after his workday is over. He seems to be still in it as he leaves the office building, which he barely escapes, the huge golden gates of the office building are just closing as he slides his way out between them.

The Logic of the Same

In *Totality and Infinity,* Emmanuel Levinas talks about the "*way* of the same."[130] The logic of the same is the logic of totality. It is the logic that one has, that one uses to make sense of the world. The logic of the same is very useful. Many can share the same logic of the same and work together to impose it on a given social space. An office space will have a logic to it, and it will be a logic of the same. Let's give a name to a logic of the same: let's call it, after Lyotard, the logic of maximum efficiency.[131] A person who employs this logic will evaluate all things in the world around him according to the logic of efficiency. Say, the criterion of efficiency is, ultimately, that which produces the most excess money, which is the logic of the same of capitalism, in general, and of corporate businesses like the one Lloyd and Paul work at, in particular. With this criterion of efficiency, speedy, accurate typing may be considered very good, even though it is quite removed from the actual production of excess money, but its goodness nevertheless derives from the idea that eventually such efficient, proficient typing will translate into the production of excess money.

What has happened in the beginning of *After Hours* is that Lloyd has defied the logic of the same of the office space. He speaks in appropriately hushed, conspiratorial, confessional tones, because he is saying things that he knows are inappropriate in that space. He says the thing that should not be said: "I do not intend to be stuck doing this for the rest of my life." This statement debases the essential logic of the space. Paul Hackett can't hack it, cannot hear it, he immediately becomes unavailable to Lloyd, who, rejected, looks at Paul with a look of hurt and humiliation. He has been rebuked by Paul; his gesture of intimacy has been rejected. He opened himself up to Paul, which means he made himself vulnerable to rebuke. Presumably there is something about Paul that elicits his trust, that makes him think that Paul will be receptive to his confession, but he was proven wrong.

Of course, Lloyd is not really wrong about Paul. Paul longs for intimacy, longs to be true to the possibilities of the aesthetic, to be true to a counter-narrative to the logic of the office space, that surround him. As Lloyd speaks, Paul glances at this watch, the ultimate gesture of enforcement of office space logic, then turns away as though he could not care less about what Lloyd is saying. But even as he seems to uphold the logic of the office space, Paul himself slips out of it as his fugued gaze moves around that space, resting first on one then on another detail in the space around him. His gaze focuses on specific tableaus with the kind of de-contextualizing concentration with which an artist sees. Lloyd's words have, like a virus, perhaps a benign virus, wormed their way into Paul's thinking, into his consciousness, creating a crack in his logic of the same. They destabilize his totality, and hint at the possibility of an infinity that is present, available, and accessible. The opposite attitudinal stance from that of being locked in the bubble of the same is that of being open to the possibility of infinity, the openness to unlimited possibilities of meaning in the other.

Paul goes home after work, still immersed in the mood indicated by the Bach piece. We see the fruits of Paul's "totality:" an empty, spare apartment, and a phone message machine with ten message buttons, but no messages. Haunted by his fugue, Paul goes out into the night for some dinner at a local diner. He is reading Henry Miller's *Tropic of Cancer*. It is a novel about a life that is everything Paul's is not—disorderly, bohemian, full of spontaneous sex, and completely devoted to art. Paul seems to be oblivious to the presence of Marcy (Rosanne Arquette), just a table away, but she starts speaking to him. She says she loves Henry Miller, and then quotes from memory a wonderful passage from *Tropic of Cancer*: "This is not a book. This is a prolonged insult, a gob of spit in the face of Art; a kick in the pants to truth, beauty, God...Something like that." It is a gesture of intimacy. She has made herself vulnerable in several ways: she has spoken first to a complete stranger, a strange man, in a strange public place; she has confessed a love of art, and of a particular artist, a risky business in the United States; she attempts to quote from memory, which is always a little scary; and, in the end, she does seem to be a little flustered by her own brazenness. But this time Paul responds. He returns the intimacy. He is charming, and working hard to see her, to respond to her, to act as though everything she said mattered. Then, in a kind of mythic gesture, she leaves him, and she leaves him with a clue, a clue for how to find her. It is indirect, as clues are, and the pathway is opened up by an artwork. The explicit offer is a plaster-of-Paris bagel and cream cheese. The implicit offer, if he can figure it out and if he has the courage to pursue it, is, of course, her.

He does and he does and he calls her. She invites him down to where she lives, down to Soho. It is already late, he presumably has work the next day, he seems to calculate for just a moment (the power of the logic of the office space), but then he accepts the invitation with enthusiasm (the power of desire), and heads out once again into the night. At this point, the theme of the movie is pretty explicitly on the model of the *katabasis*, a descent into the underworld. There is a violent taxi ride 'down' to Soho, the accompanying music is Flamenco, a music that is meant to emerge from and to evoke the dark, passionate spirit of what the Spanish call *duende*. The cab driver has the glowing red-rimmed eyes of Charon, the boatman to hell. In the chaos of speed, wind, and swerving of the ride down, Paul loses his one piece of folding money, a twenty dollar bill, and so has nothing with which to pay the cab driver. Technically, according to the myth: if you can't pay, you can't cross. In Paul's case, he can't pay so he will not be able to leave.

What follows is a scene that Scorsese himself refers to as "the signature scene" of the film. Paul rings the doorbell for a third floor apartment. He tries the door to the foyer, but it is locked. An interesting detail is a small poster of an outline in white of a figure of a man. The figure is abstract, but it appears to be simultaneously running and responding to something with horror. It is, no doubt, a warning. Kiki Bridges (Linda Fiorentino) calls out from a window above, "Are you Paul?...Here, catch!" and throws down a huge ring of keys. They are heading right at him and he has to move out of the way to keep from getting conked by them, what could be a deadly blow given how many keys there are. As they strike the pavement there is a crack of thunder, signifying the momentousness of this event. As Scorsese says, "if he accepts the keys, the game is on."[132] He accepts the keys.

Once he gets up to the apartment, he comes upon Kiki busy at work on a papier mâché sculpture of a man. Paul says, "I like that...Very much." He recognizes that it is a kind of three dimensional version of, and then misidentifies, Edvard Munch's "The Scream." Paul calls it "The Shriek." Kiki corrects him and then sets him to work on it himself. I take Paul's recognition and appreciation of the artwork as an identification with the artwork, and his misidentification of the title as a further personalization of his identification.

Art has made several appearances so far in *After Hours*. Mozart's Symphony in D-Major accompanies the opening and closing credits. Lloyd's description of his desire for a life connected with the art world seems to set up a mood in Paul that will make him receptive to some new things. This mood is itself identified by means of a Bach "Air." Marcy quotes from a novel a passage explicitly about art and then leaves Paul a clue about how to find her via an artwork, a plaster-of-Paris bagel and cream cheese. Upon entering her apartment, Paul is confronted with an artwork that he seems to identify with, it is a papier mâché man in the pose of someone who seems to be being exposed to some terrible horror. What is the role of art here?

Art

There are two primary philosophical theories of art and beauty that I want to make an appeal to here, those of Immanuel Kant and John Dewey. In *The Critique of Pure Reason,* Kant famously gives a metaphysical description of reality that is based on two worlds. The first world is the world of our experience, the world of things as we encounter them, the world that is most accurately described by science. There is, however, there must be, according to Kant, another world, the world of things-in-themselves. This is the world of how things are independent of our experience of them. About this world science can say nothing. In the first of these worlds, the world of things as we experience them, our experience is dominated by what Kant calls "interest." That is, we evaluate everything we encounter in terms of what things can do for us, how they can augment our happiness. The dominate theoretical activity in this world might be said to be economics, how to do cost-benefit analyses, how to maximize our long term satisfaction. The second world, on the other hand, gives rise to the possibilities of human experiences that transcend mere interest, to the possibility of morality, of art, of philosophy.[133]

For Kant, we inhabit both these worlds simultaneously at all times, but we can experience only one of them at a time. It is a situation a little bit like the duck/rabbit example that Ludwig Wittgenstein refers to in *Philosophical Investigations.* As Wittgenstein points out, you can see the figure as either a duck or a rabbit, but not as both at the same time.[134]

Similarly, we can experience the world either from the perspective of interest, in which case, everything will have a price,[135] or we can experience everything from the perspective that transcends all interest, from a disinterested perspective. It is from this perspective that we experience art (as well as morality).

Capitalism encourages us to experience the world in terms of interest. It encourages us to evaluate everything we encounter in terms of a price. Capitalism is an ideology, it is a system of value that we inhabit; we are surrounded by it. We are in it, as Theodor Adorno says, "like a fish in water."[136] Presumably, if one were to ask a fish about water it would say, "Water as opposed to what?" That is, from within an ideological system, the alternatives are not apparent. It is as though we were taught from a very early age to see only the rabbit. If someone were to suggest that there was a duck there we would say, "What duck?" We are taught about capitalism, about costs, interests, exchange values, good shopping, from a very early age. Art is about the duck. Art is about a different narrative from the narrative of interest. Art is about things that are, in some sense, priceless. (That is why when people try to price art they seem to go crazy—either wildly over-valuing it, spending millions for some paint on canvas, or wildly undervaluing it, considering it worthless because it is only some scratches of paint on canvas.) In the United States and in capitalistic societies in general, the vast majority will tend to dismiss art as being useless, hence worthless. Kant would agree that it is useless, but he also thinks that art, along with morality, are the only things that are really humanly important, that really have any worth besides human beings themselves.

Art as Experience, Experience as Art

According to John Dewey, in *Art as Experience*, there are laws of nature, like the law of gravity or the laws of motion, and there is a kind of law of experience. Dewey distinguishes *an* experience from experiences in general. *An* experience is something that happens that is memorable, that is meaningful, that has its own narrative with a beginning, a middle, and an end. Not everything, not most things, that happen to us become for us *an* experience. As Dewey says, "An experience has a unity that gives it its name, *that* meal, *that* storm, *that* rupture of friendship. The existence of this unity is constituted by a single *quality* that pervades the entire experience in spite of the variation of its constituent parts."[137] An experience is characterized by "flow:" "In such experiences, every successive part flows freely, without seam and without unfilled blanks, into what ensues....In an experience, flow is from something to something. As one part leads into another and as one part carries on what went before, each gains distinctness in itself."[138] The quality of an experience, this sense of flow, is essentially aesthetic in nature. As Dewey says, "the experience itself has a satisfying emotional quality because it possesses internal integration and fulfillment reached through ordered and organized movement. This artistic structure may be immediately felt. In so far, it is esthetic."[139]

"An experience has pattern and structure, because it is not just doing and undergoing in alternation, but consists of them in relationship."[140] So what is the basic pattern and structure, the law, of *an* experience? The basic pattern involves a certain retroactive component. That is, *an* experience begins when something unusual happens to us (or when we experience something usual in an unusual way), something that puts us out of our sphere of comfort and familiarity, our logic of the same. We negotiate it with the tools we have, the knowledge that we have gained from all of the experiences we have had in the past. For an experience to become *an* experience, however, there must be a period of what Dewey calls "consummation," a period of detachment and reflection in which we make the connections between the various events that we have undergone so that they become unified. So every experience will have this pattern: an event, a process of negotiating the event, a period of consummation in which we detach and compose our negotiations into a single narrative having a particular quality. This is, for Dewey, fundamentally an aesthetic process and it is most purely experienced in the experience of art.

What are the enemies of the aesthetic? "The enemies of the esthetic are neither the practical nor the intellectual. They are the humdrum; slackness of loose ends; submission to convention in practice and intellectual procedure. Rigid abstinence, coerced submission, tightness on one side and dissipation, incoherence and aimless indulgence on the other, are deviations in opposite directions from the unity of experience."[141] Or, another way to say this is to say that the enemy of the aesthetic is our uncritical acceptance and imposition of the logic of the same. To have *an* experience, then, requires a certain amount of discipline and courage as well as imagination and understanding. One must be willing to think in new ways in order to successfully negotiate new situations. What one needs to understand, what requires a certain amount of faith, is that, if one is courageous and imaginative, meanings will emerge, you *will* have an experience.

The Plaster-of-Paris Bagel and Cream Cheese and the Papier Mâché Man

Kiki Bridges is the holder of the keys, she is the one who seems to know, and she is an artist. Her first appearance is as a voice *acousmêtre*,[142] a disembodied voice, from above, like the voice of God. The two recurring artworks in the film, the plaster-of-Paris bagel and cream cheese and the papier mâché man, are both her creations. There is, I want to say, a kind of dialectic between these two artworks. The plaster-of-Paris bagel and cream cheese is what Paul came for and he is the papier mâché man. The papier mâché man is terrified and hollow. Paul's immediate response is, basically, "I get that!" What is the papier mâché man terrified of? He is terrified of the plaster-of-Paris bagel and cream cheese.

What is the significance of the plaster-of-Paris bagel and cream cheese artwork? It plays a recurring role in the movie, which suggests that it is not just arbitrary, but meaningful. It serves as both the initial point of connection between Marcy and Paul. It is how he finds her after she leaves him in the diner. It is also the ostensible subject of their parting. After a series of mutual failures at connecting with one another, in a not incomprehensible but still weird outburst of impatience, Paul demands of Marcy to actually see a plaster-of-Paris bagel and cream cheese, since that, ostensibly, is what he came down to Soho to get.

> Paul: Where are those plaster of paris paperweights, anyway? I mean, that's what I came down here to see in the first place. Well, that's not entirely true, I came to see you, but where are
>
> the paperweights? That's what I wanna see now!
> Marcy: What's the matter?
> Paul: I said I wanna see a plaster of paris bagel and cream cheese paperweight, now cough it up.

Marcy: Right now?
Paul: Yes, right now!
Marcy: They're in Kiki's bedroom.
Paul: Then get'em, cause as we sit here chatting, there are important papers flying rampant around my apartment cause I don't have ANYTHING to hold them down with.

After this outburst by Paul, Marcy runs sobbing out of the room to Kiki's room and Paul picks up his coat and slips out of the apartment. When he returns, Marcy will be dead.

What is the source of Paul's sudden impatience? Why the sudden demand to see the plaster-of-Paris bagel and cream cheese? What is going on here? What does the plaster-of-Paris bagel and cream cheese signify? How to be delicate, but to the point? There is something decidedly pudendal about a bagel and cream cheese. Consider what a bagel and cream cheese is: it is a viscous substance around a hole. A plaster-of-Paris bagel and cream cheese is a reified, unedible, but artistic, version of that. Is this not what Marcy seems to be offering Paul? Is it not, at least from Paul's perspective, an offer to come down and see her bagel and cream cheese? There is some ambiguity here about what is being offered as well as about what Paul wants. Which is being offered and which does Paul really want, the art-version or the real, edible thing? When he makes his demand to see an actual plaster-of-Paris bagel and cream cheese, he is frustrated to the point of anger with what seems to him a perpetual postponement and deferral of what he has come down for. Although, I would say, he himself is not altogether sure what that was.

There are some ironies here. One irony is that Paul explodes at just the moment that Marcy seems to be genuinely offering herself to him sexually. That suggests a certain ambivalence on the part of Paul. It suggests that he does not really want what he thinks he wants and that his unconscious knows that and is working for his real desire. What he thinks he wants is an impersonal, low-cost sexual experience. This is a kind of infantile, solipsistic approach to sex.

Hitchcock's *Rear Window* (1954) is nicely invoked several times, a movie that also involves a sexual contretemps between a man suffering from some sexual ambivalence and a very blonde woman. First, as Paul goes up the steps to Kiki's apartment, we hear piano music reminiscent of the piano music that is being played in one of the apartments that is being watched by Jeff (James Stewart) in *Rear Window*. Later, Paul will look out Marcy's bedroom window and see two people having sex, which is the pure expression of his own fantasy and desire at that moment. Still later, fleeing a crowd after his head, he climbs a fire-escape ladder and sees into the opposite building a woman shooting a man several times. This, too, is presumably an objective correlative of the dramas of his internal fantasy space, where he feels both fear and deserving of this fate himself. Films, in general, create a sense of the oneiric, the dream-state, where our fantasies, our desires and fears, are projected and played out. As Jean Douchet says of the film spectator and of the character of Jeff in *Rear Window*, "What he sees [the spectator] on the screen (and so what Stewart watches in the apartment on the other side of the courtyard) is the projection of his own self."[143] Paul, like Jeff in *Rear Window*, feels some ambivalence about his own desires and retreats from them and their object. The Lacanian formula is that enthusiasm increases with distance and anxiety increases with proximity of the object of our desire, a fitting equation for both Paul and Jeff.[144]

So, another irony is that what Paul really wants is precisely the plaster-of-Paris bagel and cream cheese, not the real, edible version. When Marcy finally seems to be ready to offer, as it were, the real thing, it is just then that Paul seems to flip out and then flee the scene. He makes a dramatic shift from not having enough of what he wants to having way too much, the equation of enthusiasm and an anxiety à la Lacan. In support of this line of interpretation that the papier mâché man and the plaster-of-Paris bagel and cream cheese are invoking issues that have to do with male anxiety about female genitals, let me just refer to a truly horrific scene in *Taxi Driver* (1976). The scene I have in mind is the scene in which a cab passenger, played by Martin Scorsese himself, rants to Travis Bickle (Robert De Niro) about what he would like to do to his girlfriend with a .44 magnum. That scene portrays this particular male anxiety magnified to a terrifying degree, so Scorsese does have these things in mind. The question, then, is how does one appropriately negotiate a plaster-of-Paris bagel and cream cheese?

Sex

How are sex and art the same thing, as Picasso says? Both sex and art demand of us an experience. That is, both sex and art represent an encounter with an Other, an encounter with a logic that will inevitably challenge our logic of the same. Both sex and art will demand from us a transformation, an adaptation to something completely new. Both sex and art will present us with a challenge that will threaten to undo us as we are. Both sex and art will demand that we leave behind the world of interest and the simple calculus of exchange values. They will both challenge us to engage in the much more difficult logic of dealing with subjectivities, with non-fungible, hence priceless, autonomous people and artworks. The authentic encounter with an Other is always a challenge to who we are and we may not survive the encounter. As Nietzsche says, what does not kill you makes you stronger, but that suggests that sometimes things just kill you. Hence the terror we may feel at the possibility of having to have an authentic encounter with another.

One strategy is to try to avoid an *authentic* encounter with an Other. One does that by trying to impose upon the Other one's own logic of the same, by insisting that the Other conform to what one expects and wants the other to be. This happens in both sex and art. We reduce the Other to, essentially, a figure in our fantasy space, to an object (a denial of their autonomous subjectivity). This is an encounter with another that does not include authentic intercourse and so is, ultimately, fundamentally, solitary. We do this with people by refusing to acknowledge anything about them other than what we want them to be, say, available sexually in a compliant way. We do this with art in the same way, we reduce the paralogical newness and oddness of an artwork to the comfortable logic of our predetermined expectations. From this perspective, we may like the artwork or dislike the artwork, but in neither case are we really challenging ourselves to encounter the real artwork itself in all of its autonomous uniqueness.

This is the strategy Paul employs throughout *After Hours*. He is repeatedly being confronted with the paralogical, with people and artworks that challenge his logic of the same, and, except for one brief moment of open responsiveness when he first gets down to Soho and first encounters the papier mâché man, Paul becomes increasingly resistant to the appeals made upon him by people who want to be encountered, who want to be seen by him, in all of their strange difference. This persistent denial of their autonomous subjectivity will rouse the people of Soho to rise up against him, and he will stand, as a symbol, for all of society's logic of the same that denies acknowledgment of differences. Nor can Paul really be blamed. He is the product of an ideology. One strongly feels that he does not particularly want to be cruel, but somehow cannot help himself. This, I believe, is something with which many of us can identify.

How does one have a successful sexual encounter? Given that everything I have been saying indicates that an authentic encounter demands a responsiveness to the new, hence makes any formulaic prescription anathema, let me present one philosophical account of how a successful sexual encounter will go, an account that is especially appropriate to a repeated theme in *After Hours*. In his essay, "Sexual Perversion," Thomas Nagel picks up and extends a model of the sexual encounter from Jean Paul Sartre's *Being and Nothingness*, what Sartre refers to as "a double reciprocal incarnation."[145] Nagel says, "Sexual desire involves a kind of perception, but not merely a single perception of its object, for in the paradigm case of mutual desire there is a complex system of superimposed mutual perceptions—not only perceptions of the sexual object, but perceptions of oneself. Moreover, sexual awareness involves considerable self-awareness to begin with—more than is involved in ordinary sensory perception. The experience is felt as an assault on oneself by the view (or touch, or whatever) of the sexual object." This description brings in a lot of what I have been talking about with respect to authentic encounters with people (and art) in general. Self-awareness requires a certain detachment from one's immediate interests. An authentic encounter is, above all, about perception, about being able to see the other in their otherness (as opposed to imposing one's own expectations onto the other and seeing only those). A sexual encounter, then, will really only be a specialized form of what any authentic encounter with another will be like. And, like any authentic encounter, one experiences a certain element of danger, of risk, in the sexual encounter.

Nagel constructs a situation to illustrate Sartre's idea of a double reciprocal incarnation. This situation involves a series of mirrors in which two people, in a cocktail lounge, begin to notice one another. The idea that he is illustrating is that a person's (sexual) responses develop and change as they become aware of, first, the other person becoming aware of them, and, second, as they see the other person's responses begin to change and develop in response to their own developing responses. One's initial response to someone one finds attractive Nagel calls a "solitary" response. That is, the response is just about you and your own pleasure, but that response becomes reciprocal and authentic intercourse, i.e., non-solitary, when you start responding to the other person's responses.[146]

Nagel traces this development through several iterations of mutual visual awareness via the mirrors and increasing mutual, reciprocal embodiment until some further intercourse (presumably, a conversation and then later maybe even sex) ensues. The point I want to take from this, however, is that the authentic encounter will always involve some kind of mutual, reciprocal perception and responsiveness, and that in the authentic sexual encounter this will include a kind of mutual, reciprocal embodiment (which would be a difference between sex and art, Picasso's claim notwithstanding). In *After Hours,* Paul is repeatedly shown looking in mirrors at his own reflection. It is a perfect visual trope for showing his entrapment in his own logic of the same, his essential solipsism, his inability to see and respond to the other and so have his sexual arousal be anything but solitary.

My sense is that his final self-examination in a mirror, just before he goes out to dance with June in the Club Berlin is different. In that scene he is looking at himself to see how he will look to June. This is a change, this involves some detachment from himself. It is an attempt at some self-awareness. It is the potential beginning of an authentic encounter with another.

"Lies"

The original title of the script for *After Hours* by Joseph Minion was entitled "Lies." The title raises certain questions, poses certain conundrums, like who is lying to whom and when? Certainly, Paul is lying when he calls Kiki Bridges about his interest in a plaster-of-Paris bagel and cream cheese, but it is so transparent a lie and Kiki is so not fooled by it that it hardly seems to count. Marcy seems to be enacting some kind of psycho-drama about being burnt, but she never says that she has burns; and Paul has his own issues with burns which lead him to mis-recognize a tattoo on her inner thigh as a burn, so the whole thing about Marcy's burns seems way beyond any kind of simple lie. Paul explicitly accuses Marcy of lying about the pot they are smoking, but that is just a bizarre accusation which is immediately followed by Paul's meltdown about the plaster-of-Paris bagel and cream cheese. So, to what is the original title referring? On the other hand, neither Paul nor Marcy is really being straight with the other. Marcy really is burnt in the sense of just having been dumped by her boyfriend, but she never tells Paul about that and that is pretty important information for him to have for him to understand what she is thinking. He is pretending to be nicer and more interested in something other than sex than he is. This mutual dishonesty makes all of their conversations pretty painful for all involved, including for us, the audience.

For Levinas, the way totality opens itself up to infinity is through authentic conversation.[147] Conversation, from the Latin for a 'turning with', suggests a mutual reciprocal responsiveness and transformation. Authentic conversation (so, clearly, there is inauthentic conversation, faux conversation, ersatz conversation) requires, therefore, a lowering of one's guard at the totalizing borders of one's logic of the same. Authentic conversation requires a certain vulnerability, it requires that one allow the penetration and subsequent influence on one's logic of the same by alterity, by the other. Alterity, itself, is just the logic of the same of the other, and the other must simultaneously allow its own logic of the same to be influenced by your logic of the same. This is the situation of totality opening itself up to infinity. This is what authentic conversation is really about.

The experience of infinity, of another person in all their otherness, is the experience of a general paralogism. The old logics no longer apply. Space will not quite be space, time not time. Things will seem to happen by chance. Having a conversation, then, can be a dangerous business. It can also be a transcendent experience. Alterity gets transformed into, in Mark Taylor's phrase, altarity (altar-ity), something spiritual.[148] A great conversation can be as though two minds become one. (And this can even lead to a physical union, physical intercourse.) This sense of the unification of pluralities is characteristic of the sense of the spiritual. This, presumably, is what both Paul and Marcy are really after; both will fail to make such an experience possible for the other, and so will fail to achieve it for themselves.

Club Berlin

The Club Berlin functions as a kind of allegory within the story. Do not Paul's experiences with the Club Berlin recapitulate, in a different narrative form, his experiences with Marcy? He wants to get in, he tries to get in, but entrance is refused. Suddenly he gets what he wants, he gets in, but it is crazy in there, it is too much for him and he flees, as if for his life. It recapitulates the story of the Wizard of Oz as well. That too is a story of someone who wanted something, a more exciting life, and then found the reality pretty terrifying and tries to get home. *The Wizard of Oz* (1939) makes its explicit appearance in *After Hours* in the story that Marcy tells Paul about her first husband who had a thing for *The Wizard of Oz*. Apparently, at the moment of climax during sex he would yell out "Surrender Dorothy!" This was too much for Marcy and she left him. And this is just what Paul wants to yell, "Surrender Marcy!" That makes him, in this context, both like Marcy's ex-husband and something like the evil witch of the West. Of course, he is also Dorothy, someone who wished for a more exciting life, got his wish, and then only wanted to get back home again.

The first Club Berlin sequence is a recreation of Franz Kafka's short story "Before the Law."[149] In the story, there is a gatekeeper who guards the gate of the law. A man from the country comes to the gate and wants to enter, but the gatekeeper refuses him entrance. The dialogue of the bouncer at Club Berlin is right from the translation of Kafka's story. In the story, the man waits at the gate for years, always trying to gain access, until his death. At the point of his death, the man asks the gatekeeper why no one else has come to this gate and the gatekeeper tells the man that the gate was for him alone and then closes the gate. What is the law to which this gate is the entrance way? Inside the Club Berlin, illuminating the scene of chaos below from the rafters above is the figure of Martin Scorsese, another allegory within the allegory of the story.

The Gatekeeper and the Law and the "anamorphic spot"

What is the law and who is the gatekeeper? One interpretation might be that the law is simply the law of experience that Dewey describes, the law that says that in order to have an experience one must abandon one's logic of the same. In order to gain access to the realm of where the meanings are, in order to actually encounter, enter into an authentic relationship with, another person, one must open oneself up to the infinity of possible meanings of their being. This requires making oneself vulnerable to their influence. It requires thoughtful perceptions of the signals they are sending and thoughtful responses in one's own behavior to those signals. The thoughtfulness requires some detachment from one's immediate responses, since those will be coming out of one's logic of the same. What one is looking for is what Slavoj Žižek refers to as the "anamorphic spot,"[150] the things that do not fit or seem to make sense (because they point to a realm of meaning, a logic that obtains, outside your own logic of the same). The claim is that there is always an anamorphic spot, a distortion in the scene that generates, if one pays attention to it, a counter-narrative to the apparent narrative of the scene. A certain kind of attention, a certain kind of being open to the possibility that there might be more going on than first appearances suggest can help one to identify that spot. To identify the spot and to be responsive to its indications is to begin to see the deeper patterns of meaning in a situation. To see, or to understand, the deeper patterns of meaning is to be empowered, is to achieve another level of freedom, and is what it means to do philosophy.

The sheer multiplicity of invisible but operative narratives is something that has been brought much more to the forefront of the general consciousness by postmodern and multiculturalist social critiques. Feminist issues, ethnic issues, gender issues have all become much more visible to the general population, but were all once almost completely invisible to, especially, the dominant social groups (men, protestants, northern Europeans, and the upper-middleclass). Certainly, Paul's adventures in Soho immerse him in a kind of 80's WASP nightmare of multicultural empowerment where women and homosexual men seem to dominate the social spaces.

Reading signs to figure out what is really going on is something we tend not to do when we are comfortable and feel in control, but it is something that we are forced to do when confronted with things that are threatening or which make no sense to us. Good movies frequently confront us with things that do not make sense to us right away and so we are compelled to start trying to read the signs, to try to figure out the larger narrative behind the apparent facts that are being portrayed. And what we are looking for, of course, is for the anamorphic spots, the things that do not quite fit that suggest something else that might be going on. This is what philosophers are doing all the time, trying to put together some larger truth from all of the anamorphic signs that do not fit into the dominant social narratives. The narratives that we are told, that we are given cannot be right if there are all of these counter-indications, but what, then, is the true narrative? Good movies, like life itself, confront us with this deep question.

Marcy, to Paul, is like a jumble of anamorphic spots. Practically every other sentence she utters is an anamorphic spot in their conversation. That is, Marcy is constantly giving Paul mixed signals, signals that suggest two very different narratives of what she wants from him. On the one hand, she is sending signals that suggest that she is interested in having sex with him that very night. On the other hand, she is sending signals that she is deeply troubled about something and that she wants to talk to him about it, and that she really does not want to have sex with him right now at all.

In a sense, the same pattern pertains to each of the women (except Kiki

Bridges, the holder of the keys) he meets in Soho. Julie (Teri Garr) sends him what is both a cry of her own anguish, but also an echo of Paul's own inner voice, in a note saying "I hate my job." They go to her apartment and she suggests, among other things, that he touch her hair. The signals seem to be that she would like to have sex with him; the not so subtle anamorphic spots, however, are all of the mousetraps around her bed. Once again Paul feels overwhelmed by these contradictory signals. Once again he wants to flee. Once again a plaster-of-Paris bagel and cream cheese artwork is an object of potential intercourse, an object presented as a gift, that he does not know how to receive or what to do with. I take it as further evidence of the pudendal significance of the plaster-of-Paris bagel and cream cheese, that when Julie offers it to him as a reward for his return, she holds it right in front of her pelvis.

A similar encounter ensues with Gail (Catherine O'Hara). Like Julie, Gail seems to be strangely, inordinately attracted to Paul. Like Julie (like Circe and Calypso with Odysseus),[151] she tries to keep him within the island sanctuary of her apartment for herself. Gail is, ostensibly, trying to help him with his bleeding arm and with a phone so that he can call someone to come get him and get him out of Soho. Her ingenious method of undoing this help is to recite arbitrary numbers as he tries to dial the number he gets from directory assistance. Again, there are clearly mixed signals being sent by Gail and Paul receives them in sheer disbelief. He responds badly which makes Gail a little edgy, not a thing one wants Gail to be once one gets to know Gail better. She discovers and reads an oracular piece of newspaper stuck to Paul's shoulder from his work helping Kiki with her papier mâché statue. The news story recounts a terrible mob attack on a man in which they collectively beat him to death, and, according to the story, pummel his face beyond recognition. Gail says, "Whoa! What does a guy have to do to get his face pummeled?" Paul, and we, the audience, have the distinct sense that this story may be about him somehow, but what the answer to Gail's question is, that is, what exactly it is that he has done to deserve such treatment, remains unclear. Interestingly, within moments, Gail will be at the head of a mob that seems intent on doing just what was recounted in the story to Paul. Whatever it is that Paul is guilty of, Gail seems to feel herself a victim of it.

Each of the people that Paul encounters in Soho offer him the possibility of intimacy, the possibility of an experience. It is almost as though Paul himself were a kind of walking, talking anamorphic spot. Each person he encounters seems to see in him the possibility of a genuine encounter, the possibility of a genuine conversation. This is exactly what Paul is looking for as well; it is why he is in Soho, although it is not clear that he knows this about himself. It seems like he may think he is there for something like easy sex. That is not what he really wants or really needs and, in this case, others seem to understand this about him better than he understands this about himself. He is trying to keep his attention, first, on sex, then, later, on escape, but these are misinterpretations of his own desires. What he really wants is intercourse, intercourse which may include sex, but is not limited to or, ultimately, only about sex.

Time

A question is raised about time in *After Hours*. The title itself raises the question: What is 'after hours' time? Time is a very tricky subject. As Augustine says in his *Confessions*, "What then is time? Provided that no one asks me, I know. If I want to explain it to an inquirer, I do not know."[152] Time seems to have a dual metaphysical aspect, much like Kant's description of the world in general. The classic expression of this contrast occurs in the contrasting conceptions of ancient Greek time, the kronos/kairos distinction. Kronos time is the tick tock time of everyday busyness. Capitalism is all about Kronos time. As Michel Foucault describes in *Discipline and Punish*, capitalism gives rise to what he calls "disciplinary space" and "disciplinary time."[153] Kronos is a form of disciplinary time, a discipline enforced in our Western world by means of a proliferation of clocks and watches. Kairos time is associated with heroic time, time that feels fluid, infinite, outside of time. In kairos time, a minute can seem like an hour, and an hour pass by as if it were a minute. When Mihaly Csikszentmihalyi talks about "flow,"[154] he is talking about what I understand kairos time to be, and nicely connects Dewey's idea about having an experience, his idea of the aesthetics of experience, with kairotic time.

"Flow" occurs when the activity we are doing is matched in difficulty to our abilities, so that it takes all of our skill and concentration to perform the activity, but, in devoting all of that energy, we are successful at the activity. Flow is a kind of hyper-drive during which time is completely relativized. The absence of flow ontologizes time, makes it a veritable physical presence, heavy and obdurate. Maximum satisfaction is experienced during flow conditions. To achieve flow is an art. It transcends mere efficiency; there are no rules for how to get there. It takes training, skill, practice, knowledge and a complete, honest immersion in the activity itself. When flow is achieved, the activity is not just satisfying, it feels meaningful. Of course, flow can be experienced in seduction as well. If the seduction is not going well, time slows and oppresses. Paul is no expert at it, and so the clock keeps ticking.

There is an additional component to kairos time that does not belong to kronos time, there is an ethical dimension to it. In kairos time, one is doing what Aristotle is advocating in the *Nicomâchéan Ethics,* that is, one is in the groove of doing the right thing at the right time for the right reason. Kairos time, for example, makes an appearance in Plato's *Phaedrus*. The first speech that Socrates gives he will later describe as a-kairotic.[155] It is a speech that is a bad speech that was given at the wrong time for the wrong reasons. Socrates tries to correct this perversion of time and speech by presenting a kairotic speech, a speech that is true, heartfelt, appropriate, and timely.

Paul is not really a bad person, but he does not really know himself and he does not really know what he is doing, and so he does things badly. This "badly" has both a practical component, he is not very good at getting what he wants, and an ethical component, everyone he encounters seems to suffer from the encounter with him. The question, then, is how can he become better, how can he be a better person?

The End

The ending of the movie is even more surreal, if that is possible, than the surreality that has come before it. There is one theological moment in the film, perhaps a reference to the aborted *Last Temptation of Christ*, when Paul falls to his knees, looks up into the night sky and cries, "What do you want from me?" It is a moment in which Paul explicitly acknowledges the limits of his own powers, the uselessness of his own logic, and his sense of larger patterns at work. It is a moment that will make possible the beginnings of his redemption. Chased by the maenads (which makes him a kind of proto-Orpheus), who really do seem to want to simply tear him to pieces, he flees to Club Berlin, a club to which he failed to get free access earlier in the movie. He had gone there earlier looking for Kiki Bridges and, presumably, that is why he is returning there now, but this time he has an invitation flier to get him in, an invitation to a Conceptual Art Party at Club Berlin.

When Paul gets to Club Berlin this time, everything is different. Where he could not gain access to the door previously, this time, he is let immediately in, as though the door were just for him (as it is in Kafka's story). When he gets inside the place is virtually empty, just the barkeeper and an older woman sitting by herself at a table, drinking from a silver cup. Paul is not the same person he was at the beginning of the movie.[156] His confident arrogance, along with his easy boredom, have been stripped from him. He is on the run for his very life, and in the process of running he seems to have discovered that he wants to live. He goes to the older woman, June (Verna Bloom), and offers himself to her. It is a desperate, vulnerable, sincere offering. She receives it as a gift, but it will be she who has the gift to give to him, the gift of life, the gift of art. His trials have finally rendered him able to give a gift, made him able to really see another person in her loneliness and pain, and so be seen by another person in his loneliness and pain. He will need her help when the Bacchants come beating at the door, looking for his head, and she will help him. She will turn him into a work of art, an artwork of a tormented man cringing at his fate. He will become externally what he has for a long time been internally. That is not what the Maenads are looking for and they will be deceived.

Each form of reality contains the anamorphic spots that, if attended to, open up to that reality's contrary. What is needed is a way of mapping the landscapes of these various realities. Art will provide the doorways through to alternate realities, but it will take philosophy to get a perspicuous overview of the landscapes, to map the interrelations of the various realities. The meanings emerge only in the transitions. Without the transitions, we are locked in our logics of the same. We see new relations, new meanings, when we make the transitions, when the reality we inhabit gets transformed. This seeing is an ethics, an ethics in Aristotle's sense of something that empowers and emancipates, while simultaneously connecting us to others and to the larger social whole. This is the way life itself becomes meaningful.

Apparently, Scorsese was uncertain about how to end the movie *After Hours*, but the ending he settled on seems right. The Paul Hackett sculpture falls out of the back of a careening van and breaks open before the golden gates of his very own office building. This certainly seems to be a kind of rebirth from the womb of art. Paul dusts himself off, enters the building, goes to his desk, and sits before his computer which greets him with, "Good morning, Paul." The camera tracks around the office space as it did at the beginning of the movie. People are coming in, ready to start a new business day. Weirdly, as the camera tracks back and passes by Paul's desk, he is no longer there. Gone to another plane of reality—perhaps, a lesson, perhaps, for us all.

Section Three

Neo-Westerns

6 | Regeneration through Stories and Song:
The View from the Other Side of the West in Chris Eyre's *Smoke Signals*

The educational journey of modern Indian people is one spanning two distinct value systems and worldviews. It is an adventure in which the Native American sacred view must inevitably encounter the material and pragmatic focus of the larger American society. In that meeting ground lies an opportunity for the two cultures to both teach and learn from each other.

—Vine Deloria in his Preface to *Power and Place: Indian Education in America*

What is it that makes a Western a Western? Is a Western a Western because of where it is situated? Is the West of a Western a place or a plot or an attitude or is it some still vaguer concept that includes all of these, but is reducible to none? By location, *Smoke Signals* is certainly a Western, but location seems an especially insufficient criterion for identifying what makes a Western a Western. Richard Slotkin, in his book *Regeneration through Violence: The Mythology of the American Frontier 1600-1860*, argues that the myth of the West is the founding myth of the American identity. He speaks of the founding fathers in "the American mythogenesis" as those "who tore violently a nation from the implacable and opulent wilderness."[157] Included in this "implacable and opulent wilderness" were the indigenous people of the land, and so they were part of the violence, the subjects of the violence, that brought forth the new nation. Slotkin says, "Myth describes a process…by which knowledge is transformed into power; it provides a scenario or prescription for action, defining and limiting the possibilities for human response to the universe."[158] The same could be said of stories in general. If the traditional Westerns, novels and films, are part of the founding myth of the American identity, what role does, or can, a story from the other side of the myth, a story about indigenous people, told by and from the perspective of indigenous people, play? *Smoke Signals* (Chris Eyre, 1998) is such a story, the first feature film that was written, directed, and co-produced by Native Americans. The question is a philosophical one, and it will take some philosophy to answer it.

Bruce Wilshire, in his *The Primal Roots of American Philosophy: Pragmatism, Phenomenology, and Native American Thought*, finds, as his title suggests, the roots of American pragmatism, the unique philosophical contribution to world philosophy by America, in Native American thought. As Wilshire says of pragmatism, "*It is original because it is aboriginal.*"[159] Both Emerson and Thoreau had many encounters with Native Americans and both were deeply impressed with Native American ways of regarding and thinking about Nature. Insofar as Emerson and Thoreau are responsible for writing our founding intellectual texts, as such contemporary philosophers as Cornell West and Stanley Cavell have argued,[160] they are also responsible for constructing some important elements of our American identity. That American identity as it is articulated in Emerson's and Thoreau's Transcendentalism and then later in the pragmatism of Peirce, James, and Dewey, is profoundly inclusive, strives always for ways to sustain a relationship with complexity, is non-dogmatic, and has as its constant aim the amelioration of pain and suffering. At the same time, it is also an expression of the American character that has treated its indigenous people with such terrible violence and cruelty. This tension in the American identity comes to the fore when we consider the movie *Smoke Signals* as a part of the genre of the Western.

Smoke Signals is composed of several overlapping and interweaving stories, but the core story is of the journey made by Victor Joseph (Adam Beach) and Thomas Builds-the-Fire (Evan Adams) to recover the truck and cremated remains of Victor's father, Arnold Joseph (Gary Farmer). They are Coeur d'Alene Indians living on the Coeur d'Alene reservation in Idaho. Arnold's remains are outside Phoenix, Arizona, where Arnold moved when he abandoned his family. Neither Victor nor his mother, Arlene Joseph (Tantoo Cardinal), have enough money to pay for his trip down to Phoenix, and that is how Thomas gets to go along. Thomas has saved enough coins and bills to pay for the trip and offers it to Victor on the condition that he, Thomas, go along with him. Victor is resistant to that suggestion, there have been tensions between the two since early childhood, but finally he relents.

Fire and Smoke

The movie begins and ends with fire. Fire is the primary trope for the violence that is both perpetrated and suffered by all the major characters in the movie. It is also the primary trope for the possibility of regeneration. Although Victor seems to be the protagonist of the film, it is Thomas Builds-the-Fire that is at the center of this trope of fire, since it was his parents who had the huge house party, on the fourth of July, which ended in fire. It is also Thomas Builds-the-Fire who, through his stories, will construct a narrative of redemption and regeneration that will be transformative for all.

Smoke signals are signals of distress, a form of communication that is designed to cross great distances. Of course, there are great distances to be communicated across, between Thomas and Victor; between Victor and his father, Arnold; between the reservation and the white world through which Victor and Thomas must travel to get to Arnold's remains; between the Native American world, in general; and the world of non-tribal America, to which the movie *Smoke Signals* is also meant to appeal. Sherman Alexie, who wrote the book the movie is based on as well as the screenplay for the movie, says the following of his choice of "smoke signals" for the title of his screenplay:

> *Smoke Signals* fits for a number of reasons, for me. On the surface, it's a stereotypical title, you think of Indians in blankets on the plains sending smoke signals, so it brings up a stereotypical image that's vaguely humorous. But people will also instantly recognize that, in a contemporary sense, smoke signals are about calls of distress, calls for help. That's really what this movie is about—Victor, Thomas, and everybody else calling for help. It's also about the theme of fire. The smoke that originates from the second fire brings about the beginning of resolution. So I just thought *Smoke Signals* worked very poetically.[61]

There is a scene early in the movie in which the young Victor and the young Thomas are warming themselves around a fire in a barrel. Thomas is talking to Victor, but Victor is not responding. Thomas is talking about the colors of things that are revealed in fire, and then mentions that he has heard that Victor's father is living in Phoenix, Arizona. Cruelly, Victor says, "What color do you think your mom and dad were when they burned up?" In the screenplay, although not in the movie, Thomas continues on the theme of Victor's father, and finally asks, "What does Phoenix, Arizona, mean?"[162] The figure of the phoenix exactly captures this idea of fire as element of destruction and regeneration. In the voice-over Thomas describes Victor and himself as children of fire and ash. It is a reference to the violence that both have suffered from, and to the regeneration both will need and seek.

Western Movies from the Native Persepective

There is a scene on the bus that Victor and Thomas are taking down to Phoenix in which Victor gets exasperated with Thomas' constant storytelling and says, "I mean, you just go on and on talking about nothing. Why can't you have a normal conversation? You're always trying to sound like some damn medicine man or something. I mean, how many times have you seen *Dances with Wolves*? A hundred, two hundred times?"[163] Part of the joke is that Thomas *has* seen the movie that many times. So, there is a tragi-comedy right there: a young Native American man learning how to be Native American by means of a movie made by Kevin Costner. That tragi-comedy is compounded when we understand Slavoj Žižek's pointed critique of *Dances with Wolves* (Kevin Costner, 1990). Žižek compares *Dances with Wolves* to another movie from 1990, *Awakenings* (Penny Marshall). What the two movies have in common, according to Žižek, is a surface, official content and a latent, unofficial (but the real) content, which Žižek explains in terms of a principle of symbolic exchange. The official content of the movies is about the relationship between a doctor and his coma stricken patients (*Awakenings*) and the relationship between a Civil War lieutenant and a tribe of Lakota Sioux Indians (*Dances with Wolves*). The real content of these movies, according to Žižek, is the creation of the couple, so that the real significance of the coma patients and the Indians is only to make possible the sexual relationship of the healthy white men. As Žižek says, "In *Dances with Wolves*, the role of the group of patients is taken over by the Sioux tribe which is also allowed to disappear in an implicit symbolic exchange, so that the couple of Kevin Costner and the white woman who has lived among the Indians since childhood can be produced."[164]

On the one hand, it is a pretty sad state of affairs, if also funny, when an young Indian man chooses to learn about being an Indian from a Kevin Costner film. On the other hand, there is another Hollywood movie made by non-Indians that was very influential on Sherman Alexie and Chris Eyre, and that movie is *Little Big Man* (1970), from a novel by Thomas Berger and directed by Arthur Penn. Alexie has explicitly acknowledged the influence of *Little Big Man* on his writing of *Smoke Signals* and there are probably more references to the earlier movie than I can understand, but two are pretty explicit. The first is the repeated reference, with variations, to the phrase first enunciated by Old Lodge Skins (Chief Dan George) in *Little Big Man*, "It's a good day to die." That phrase becomes, in *Smoke Signals*: "Sometimes it's a good day to die. Sometimes it's a good day to play basketball." and "Sometimes it's a good day to die, and sometimes it's a good day to eat at Denny's."

The other, to me, clear reference is to the "contrary," Younger Bear (Cal Bellini), in *Little Big Man*. A "contrary" among the Human Beings (what the Cheyenne called themselves in the movie) was one who does everything backwards, saying goodbye when they mean hello or hello when they mean goodbye, or washing with dirt and drying themselves off with water. The contraries in *Smoke Signals* are Velma and Lucy, who drive all over the reservation backwards, and, at one point, give Victor and Thomas a ride in exchange for a story. Their names, Velma (Michelle St. John) and Lucy (Elaine Miles), are themselves references to the movie *Thelma and Louise* (Ridley Scott, 1991), a movie about two women who also do some crazy driving. I think Alexie and Eyre want us to laugh at the influence of *Dancing with Wolves* on Thomas, with, basically, something like Žižek's critique in mind, and to see the positive influence of *Little Big Man* on *Smoke Signals*. This is a very pragmatic move. It is a form of cultural critique that is undogmatic and ameliorative. The point is that being influenced by non-Native movies is not necessarily bad, or that all movies made by non-Indians are bad, but that some movies made by non-Indians may do a kind of unperceived violence, and that that violence may best be got at with humor. In general, *Smoke Signals* deals with violence with humor, a humor that is tinged with sadness, which seems to be very characteristic of Native American thinking, in general.

Tribal and Non-Tribal

The early Americans were influenced by Native American practices according to Slotkin in *Regeneration through Violence*. As Slotkin says, "We know that the colonists adapted their ways of living, farming, hunting, and fighting in order to survive in the Indians' world."[165] Slotkin suggests that the colonists learned their adaptations from the Indians. Slotkin goes on to ask the question, "Did they [the colonists] also (to some degree) acquire an Indian-like vision of the New World...?" Slotkin's long, attenuated answer to this question seems to be, basically, no. Near the end of his book Slotkin provides this contrast between "the tribesman" and the "white hunter":

> For the tribesman, wilderness life, notwithstanding its requirement of hunting, was one of community rather than solitude. For the Indian the wilderness was home, the locus of the tribe that was the center of his metaphysical universe as well as his social existence. Even in moments of physical solitude, on a long hunt or a vision quest, the world community about him remained intact, for the gods and the wild animals were his fellows and kin. The border of tribal solidarity extended out from the village center to the edges of creation. The white hunter was an alien, paradoxically achieving a sense of relation to the world through an ordeal of profound physical, moral, and psychological isolation from society. His destiny was personal rather than tribal; his moral obligation was to himself, his "gifts," and his racial character, rather than to his fellows and his environment.[166]

In this passage quoted above from Slotkin, he refers to the center of the white hunter's moral universe being "himself, his 'gifts.'" This reference to 'gifts', and how one thinks about gifts structures one's world view, opens up a way of contrasting the two world views, that of the tribal Indians versus that of the white colonists, in general (Westerner and Easterner alike). I want to argue that the Westerner, in *some* ways, has more in common with the Easterner, is, in fact, just a more savage form of the Easterner, than he has with the tribal Indians.

To return to Lewis Hyde's *The Gift*, he contrasts gift economies with commodity or market economies. Tribal cultures tend to be oriented around gift economies whereas non-tribal cultures tend to be oriented around commodity or market economies. Ethical value in gift economies is based largely on how much a person gives away, whereas ethical value in market economies tends to accrue to the person who is able to accumulate or get the most.[167] Hyde associates gift economies with the basic principle of eros, while commodity economies are associated with logos.[168] Eros is a principle of connection, relationship, attraction, whereas logos is a principle of autonomy, distance, distinction. Both of these economies are, according to Hyde, economies of exchange. Both of these two economies generate a surplus, a remainder. In the gift economy, the remainder is the creation and sustaining of relationships, while in the commodity economy the surplus that is generated is capital.[169]

The advantage of the gift economy to the individual that lives within it is that one has a large, supportive network of relationships in which one lives and which supports one in everything one does. This network of relationships gives meaning to one's life. The downside of the gift economy is that one lives within a large network of relationships, with all of the attendant responsibilities and moral constraints that such relationships demand. The advantages of living within commodity economy are several: one is able, through capitalistic exchange, to secure a surplus of non-perishable capital that can provide security for the future. In addition, within the exchange relationship one's autonomy is maintained. Thus, no burdensome attendant moral or relational responsibilities are entailed other than the very basic ones that will guarantee sufficiently good relations to continue the exchange relationship in the future. The downside of the commodity economy of capitalist exchange is that deep relationships are not formed, there is a consequent lack of connection with other people, and people must live with a pervasive sense of alienation from other people.

One way, then, of contrasting the worldview of the tribal Indians and the non-tribal whites is to say that the tribal Indians operate within a gift economy, whereas the non-tribal whites operate within a commodities economy. The moral consequences of these two ways of living will be that the tribal Indians will tend to value relationships above all else, whereas the non-tribal whites will tend to value autonomy and the accumulation of capital over all else. This is part of the significance of Thomas saying to Victor near the end of the movie, "who needs money on the rez anyways?"[170] As I mentioned earlier, within commodity or market economies there can be smaller gift economies, social groups, such as a family or church; and in tribal communities, the people of the tribe will frequently have more of a commodity economy relationship with people outside their tribe.

Hyde contrasts gift property with commodity property in terms of movement and stasis: "The only essential is this: *the gift must always move*. There are other forms of property that stand still, that mark a boundary or resist momentum, but the gift keeps going."[171] That is, the gift economy depends on a constant circulation of gifts. Hyde refers to gifts as "anarchist property" because their possession is defined in terms of their being given up, re-circulated, and passed on to someone else. If one simply retains a gift without re-circulating it, it loses its status as a gift and becomes a mere commodity. It is this de-spiritualization of gifts, of property, that, according to Hyde, the Indian wars were about. The war "that the American Indians had to fight with the Europeans" was "a war against the marketing of formerly inalienable properties. Whereas before a man could fish in any stream and hunt in any forest, now he found there were individuals who claimed to be the owners of these commons."[172]

As Hyde points out, tribal people will not only have a gift economy among themselves, or with other tribes. They can also have a gift economy with nature itself, where there are exchanges of gifts between, as it were, the tribe, or certain tribal members, and nature. The classic example of this that Hyde refers to is that of the hunt. The deer that is killed is considered a gift from nature and the hunter, individually, or the tribe, communally, will return some portion of that gift back to nature to maintain the health of the gift cycle.[173]

The originating gift in *Smoke Signals* was the potlatch-like super party thrown by the parents of Thomas Builds-the-Fire. It is, not insignificantly, I think, a Fourth of July celebration. Tribal wisdom about technology and change is, as Gregory Cajete explains, essentially conservative. "Because social value is gained by honoring mutual reciprocal relationships, spin-offs of Native science in technology are carefully applied. Adoption of technology is conservative and based on intrinsic need, and care is taken to ensure that technologies adopted and applied do not disrupt a particular ecology."[174] A wisdom that seeks relationship, harmony, and balance will be leery of the de-stabilizing effects of the intrusion of the new. It is hard to imagine more de-stabilizing intrusions of the new than those new things that the Fourth of July commemorates, the new government of the white Europeans (creating reservations for the Indians), gunpowder (fireworks), and alcohol. The delicate balance that the potlatch is designed to uphold and celebrate gets horribly destroyed with these intrusive 'technologies' introduced by the white Europeans.

There is a kind of alternate metaphysics that is associated with a gift economy that is well described by the American Indian Vine Deloria. In his essay "American Indian Metaphysics," Deloria says,

> The best description of the Indian metaphysics was that realization that the world, and all its possible experiences, constitutes a social reality, a fabric of life in which everything had the possibility of intimate knowing relationships because, ultimately, everything was related. This world was a unified world, a far cry from the disjointed and sterile world painted by western science.[175]

This metaphysics of universal relationship is very similar to the pragmatic vision of the universe in the philosophy of Charles Sanders Peirce. In his essay, "The Law of Mind," Peirce describes the law of relationships in terms of the law of mind, which is "that ideas tend to spread continuously and to affect certain others which stand to them in a peculiar relation of affectability."[176] The law of relationships, the law of mind, is the law of the spread of influence through relationships. The spread of influence occurs in nature, in natural systems, as well as in human social systems, and so for Peirce, mind operates in nature as well as in human beings. To be aware of the directions of this spread is to understand what Peirce calls the "personality" of a particular system, and so that the world as a whole can be said, insofar as it manifests this spread throughout, to have a personality.[177]

There is a continuum of relationships. Signs of this continuum are made manifest by the spread of influence, just as the continuous surface of water may manifest itself in the action of waves. Another sign of the continuum is the nature of time, the way there is a continuity in time between past, present, and future. Peirce represents this continuity in terms of the 'insistence,' across time, of an idea. A past idea increases in its level of 'insistence' as it more closely approaches the present. Similarly, the insistence of a future idea is most powerful the closer it is to the present, and wanes in power as it fades into the more and more distant future. Furthermore, there is a continuity between past and future ideas, as Peirce says, "The future is suggested by, or rather is influenced by the suggestions of, the past."[178]

This idea of the real continuity of time is beautifully represented in *Smoke Signals*. Real, but latent or background, continuities between past, present, and future are powerfully made manifest and foregrounded via montage, the linking of one scene with the next. The general pattern is that a temporal portal is portrayed via a traditional spatial portal, a door or a window. The young Victor will walk into a doorway, and the adult Victor will walk out of a doorway, or the adult Victor will look out a window and the young Victor will appear outside that window. In this manner, the movie suggests that there are deep lines of connection between the past and the future. The present is the moment in which some kind of reconciliation, some kind of balance can be achieved between the events of the past and the potentialities of the future. The relationships that must be balanced are not just interpersonal, but inter-temporal as well.

The primary mode of conveying important understanding about the universe for American Indians is through stories. In western science, knowledge tends to be propositional, whereas native wisdom tends to be narrative in structure. The western scientist will kill a bird and cut it open to see how it works.[179] What the western scientist is looking for are the general mechanisms that explain how the bird functions. The American Indian will live with the bird, attentive especially to an individual bird's anomalous behaviors, in order to understand the personality of a particular bird, as well as learning some generalities about this bird species. This Indian way requires being responsive to anomalies, the particulars of things, special circumstances, and unusual events.[180] Understanding is constituted narratively, which is to say, through descriptions of relationships, interactions, developments, and conclusions. Since these narratives are essentially about relationships, they inevitably carry a certain ethical weight. That is, the acknowledgment of the reality of these relationships demands a certain respect for them.

The awareness of an underlying relational element is especially reinforced in Native American thinking because of their social system of clans. A person is born not just into a family, but also into a clan. A person's clan connections are often quite far reaching, both in distance and in terms of the variety of people with whom a person is connected. From the very beginning of one's life, one is raised within a large system of underlying connections and relationships that one is taught to observe and respect. One's very identity is relationally determined through one's clan. Furthermore, there is always a story about the origins of a clan, and a clan's origins will connect the clan to a specific animal. Hence there is a direct link between one's identity and the natural, non-human (that is, from the western, scientific perspective) world, and the relationships that exist there, in the animal world, as well.

One of the distinctive features of gift economies is that they are structured and maintained by stories. Since they are fundamentally relational, those relations must be systematized and communicated among the members of those economies, and that is done via stories. So stories, in tribal gift economy societies, serve an absolutely necessary and essential function. They are not mere entertainment, but contain all the most important information and knowledge that sustain the community. The most important knowledge in tribal societies is not propositional knowledge like that produced by western science, but accounts of networks of relations that situate and give meaning to each individual entity within that network of relations. The 'bad' is when the system of relations is disrupted or breaks down. The 'good' is when the system of relations is maintained or restored. Stories are the primary means of repair.

Stories

"Smoke Signals" begins with stories. It begins with, and is permeated by, and is, of course, itself, a story. The stories are about underlying relationships. They are about submerged narrative lines that are making their way to the surface. It is about latent stories becoming manifest stories, but for such stories to become manifest, someone has to listen. Part of the narrative of this story is how valuable stories are and how difficult it is to get people to listen.

When Victor Joseph is confused about what to do because he has just learned that his father has died far away in Phoenix, Arizona, and he has no money to go there, and Thomas Builds-The-Fires has offered him some money to go, but only on the condition that Victor takes him, which Victor does not want to do, he goes to his mother for advice. She tells him a story:

> You know, people always tell me I make the best fry bread in the world. Maybe it's true. But I don't make it by myself, you know? I got the recipe from your grandmother, who got it from her grandmother. And I listen to people when they eat my bread, too. Sometimes, they might say, "Arlene, there's too much flour," or "Arlene, you should knead the dough a little more." I listen to them. And I watch that Julia Child all the time.[181]

This story captures a lot of what I have been describing as core elements of American Indian philosophy. It is wisdom presented in a narrative form, as a story. It strongly emphasizes the ideas of connection, relationship, and respect. It has a definite ethical dimension. And, interestingly, amusingly, it points to an underlying holism with respect to the Julia Child reference. Wisdom and understanding can come from various sources. Wisdom is not an Indian thing or a white thing—it is a thing of the world and one must be responsive to it in all its forms, in all the ways it may come to one. This story is also very Peircean. For Peirce, truth does not belong to an individual, but emerges out of a community of inquirers. The essential components of that community are that the members of the community are interdependent, and they must experiment, and they must communicate with each other. Arlene does not tell Victor what to do. She gives him a story.

That she presents the information that she has to give in the form of a story is both an effective way of conveying all of the complex information that she has to convey (a whole worldview of information) as well as being a gesture of respect toward Victor. It signals not just her respect for his intelligence, that he will understand the point of the story, but it also respects his right to form his own judgment on the matter. A story is not coercive in the same way that 'advice' is. Victor, in turn, will hold up his end of this relationship, by understanding what the story is about and letting its wisdom guide him in making his decision.

A final, but essential, component to this story is its humor. It is a very positive, inclusive humor that simultaneously promotes intimacy and harmony in the relationship, while it also warns and provides information about more (depending on others for help) and less (signing papers with white people) effective ways of going forward in the world. Humor is not just an interpersonal phenomenon, but a spiritual phenomenon as well. As Maureen E. Smith says in her essay, "Crippling the Spirit, Wounding the Soul: Native American Spiritual and Religious Suppression:" "Many tribes saw the need for humor in all of their most sacred ceremonies. It was often an integral part of religious ceremonies."[182]

Another aspect of Native American philosophy is an emphasis on being in harmony with one's environment. This is not a different aspect so much as a different point of emphasis, since stories and song are ways of achieving that harmony. The idea of harmony here is not a notion of stasis, but is defined in terms of "completing relationships." As Vine Deloria says, "The spiritual aspect of knowledge about the world taught the people that relationships must not be left incomplete. There are many stories about how the world came to be, and the common themes running through them are the completion of relationships and the determination of how this world should function."[183]

Deloria gives the equation: power + place = Personality. This is essentially the same equation that Peirce gives for 'personality'. Deloria goes on to say, "This equation simply means that the universe is alive, but it also contains within it the very important suggestion that the universe is personal and, therefore, must be approached in a personal manner."[184] Peirce comes to the same conclusion, and, in fact, insists that anyone who really lets their mind go, who lets their mind 'muse', will come to the same conclusion.[185] This is not mysticism. It is the acknowledgment that power and place inevitably yield a kind of directional flow, yield a certain trajectory to a situation, and to know the direction of that flow, the general trajectory of that situation, is to understand the personality of that place. In this way, scientific method will continue to prove inferior to the methods of American Indian philosophy as long as the methods of science refuse to acknowledge this personality aspect to the world.

Deloria goes on to say about the importance of completing relationships, "Completing the relationship focuses the individual's attention on the results of his or her actions. Thus, the Indian people were concerned about the products of what they did, and they sought to anticipate and consider all possible effects of their actions."[186] To be in a position to be so present to the moment, so alert to "all possible effects" of one's actions, requires that one be present to oneself. In addition to the power of stories to situate a person within a context and to make manifest the relationships that obtain, American Indians also makes use of chants and song.

Abandoned Relationships and the Gifts that Heal Them

Smoke Signals is all about relationships that have been abandoned before they were completed. Victor's dad runs out on his family, but his drinking had been an impediment to complete relationship with his family for years before he finally left. The young Victor most painfully feels the uncompleted relationship with his father, and expresses his despair at this by first responding to his dad's question, "Who is your favorite Indian?" with "Nobody!" and later breaking all of the remaining beer bottles against his father's truck. Arlene, witnessing Victor's despair, and in frustration and anger at the uncompleteable relationship with Arnold, all but drives him out. Victor, as a consequence, lives with the uncompleted relationship with his father, and will not allow the completion of relationship with Thomas, or anyone else. Arnold is a kind of 'Nobody,' a man lost to himself, as well as to those he loves, a man committed to making himself 'disappear.'

In *Smoke Signals,* gifts function much more in the way of the world-view of interdependency. Thomas's gifts are his stories, as is Arlene's gift to Victor with her story about making fry bread. Arnold, bereft of himself, is bereft of gifts, and can only leave and, in the end, leave the gift of his own longing for home. Velma and Lucy, well-versed in the ways of the gift economy will give the gift of a ride for the gift of a story, which Thomas promptly provides. Victor has learned only the version of being bereft of gifts from his dad's leaving, but with Thomas's help, and with what Suzy Song (Irene Bedard) steers him to see in what his dad has left for him, he learns the way of gifts as affirmations of relationships. He gives gifts of life. He saves the woman in the car accident by going for help. He shares Arnold's remains with Thomas. And finally, when Thomas asks him if he ever found out why his dad left, he tells Thomas, "He didn't mean to." That is both the truth, which is a gift, and a withholding of a part of the truth, the information that it was because he had killed Thomas's parents by starting the fire that consumed their home. That, as Sherman Alexie says, "That is, by far, the greatest gift Victor could give Thomas."[187]

Regeneration through Song

The scene on the bus when Thomas and Victor have been evicted from their seats, or, rather, their seats have been co-opted by a couple of white men, recapitulates in miniature much of the history of white-Indian relations in America. They relocate to the back of the bus. That is what they are forced to do; what they choose to do is begin a chant. The chant is about John Wayne's teeth and how you never really see them, and what they may really be like. The chant functions to realign certain forces for the two characters. They have been thrown into a situation in which they are in conflict with their environment by the meanness of the two white men. They achieve a kind of re-attunement with their environment through song. It is an alternative to a direct confrontation, and yet reveals a remarkably sensitive insight into the dynamics of white-Indian confrontations. That is, their chant affirms their connection with an aesthetic, harmonic relationship with the world, while simultaneously observing the lack of a sense of the aesthetic in the unsmiling white men, with John Wayne as the paradigmatic example. The chant works for Victor and Thomas not unlike the way the process of musement works in Peirce's philosophy, that is, as a way of making oneself receptive to an understanding of the deeper lines of relationship and personality in a given context.

A final scene from the movie that I would like to consider is the final poem-like monologue recited in a voice-over by Thomas as he pours the ashes of Arnold Joseph into the Spokane Falls. The theme of the poem is "How do we forgive our fathers." It goes:

> How do we forgive our fathers...? Maybe in a dream?
>
> Do we forgive our fathers for leaving us too often or forever
> When we were little?
> Maybe for scaring us with unexpected rage
> Or making us nervous because there never seemed to be any rage there at all?
>
> Do we forgive our fathers for marrying or not marrying our mothers?
> For divorcing or not divorcing our mothers?
>
> And shall we forgive them for their excesses of warmth or coldness?
> Shall we forgive them for pushing or leaning? For Shutting doors?
> For speaking through walls or never speaking, or never being

silent?

Do we forgive our fathers in our age or in theirs?
Or in their deaths saying it to them or not saying it?

If we forgive our fathers, what is left?

As we hear these words we see the turbulent waters of the river as they flow beneath the bridge. I take this scene to be quite complicated, the river representing various different fluidities, manifesting various different currents and eddies of flow that correlate with various themes that occur within the movie as a whole. Time in the movie is certainly fluid and full of eddies, with portions that turn back on themselves according to certain subliminal forces, according to certain latent narratives. There is fluidity in the alignment of relationships, relationships that come into existence and seem to flow out of existence only to emerge once again later, and, perhaps looking completely different. All the relationships between the characters seem to take this form. Thomas and Victor seem inescapably bound to one another, but their acceptance of that connectedness ebbs and flows. The same could be said of the relationship between Victor and his father. The same could be said in the emerging relationship between Victor and Suzy Song.

Those who are wisest are least susceptible to this ebb and flow, and so have the most stable sorts of relationships. This seems to be true of Arlene's relationship with her son Victor, and between Thomas and his grandmother. It also seems true of the relationship between the now sober Arnold Joseph and Suzy Song. There is a sort of stability, but not stasis. The strength of those relationships depends on the mutual acceptance of growth and change in those relationships, the ability "to anticipate and consider all possible effects of their actions" on the relationships. The theme of fathers encapsulates all of these different threads. Deloria says:

> Education in the traditional setting occurs by example and not as a process of indoctrination. That is to say, elders are the best living examples of what the end product of education and life experiences shall be. We sometimes forget that life is

exceedingly hard and that no one accomplishes everything they could possibly do or even many of the things they intend to do. The elder exemplifies both the good and the bad experiences of life and witnessing their failures as much as their successes we are cushioned in our despair of disappointment and bolstered in our exuberance of success…. For some obscure reason, non-tribal peoples tend to judge their heroes much more harshly than do tribal people. They expect a life of perfection.[188]

The wisdom of American Indian philosophy and of the philosophy of Peirce seem to converge on this ethical point: that life is an ongoing experiment in which failure is as necessary a part as any success that may be achieved. The proper attitude is not the expectation of perfection, or the expectation that failure can be avoided, but to see as well as one can the interrelations that tie all things together, to try to be responsive to the flow of those relations, and to learn from the successes and failures of those that have gone before us.

This is the central teaching of pragmatism as well. We Americans are schizophrenic in the way we are torn between the demands of our market economy for autonomy and constantly more commodities and the possibilities of relationship and amelioration that our own intellectual history of pragmatism promises. We too are versions of 'Nobody' until we can find some way of resolving these tensions within us. The questions raised in the final voice-over are unanswerable questions, but the tensions they point out, the secret lines of narrative they suggest are not unlivable ones. They are about dichotomies that, in their asking, point to greater achievable unities and resolutions. It is precisely through stories and song that these tensions can be transformed into wisdom, and what better place to get a little perspective on the flow of the world, to mix narrative and song than watching a movie like *Smoke Signals*.

7 | Bad Men at Play:

On the Banality of Goodness in *Unforgiven*

Bad Men from Bodie weren't ordinary scoundrels, they came with the land, and you could no more cope with them than you could with dust or hailstones.
—E. L. Doctorow, *Welcome to Hard Times*

Clint Eastwood is not obviously a philosopher. There are, however, two parallel traditions of Western philosophy, both of which can be said to originate with Plato. One tradition, associated with the middle and later works of Plato, is the idea of philosophy as the pursuit of knowledge, which becomes for Plato, knowledge of the Forms. There is another tradition, another idea of what philosophy is about, in the earlier, the so-called Socratic, works of Plato. The idea of philosophy in those earlier works is of philosophy as a kind of wisdom, specifically, the wisdom to understand that we do not always really know what we think we know. It is this wisdom that I see Eastwood developing in *Unforgiven*. Most profoundly, what we do not know that we think we know is what we want. We think we want a certain kind of power—the power of the gun, say. The power to do whatever we want, to instill fear in others, to dominate. We want this power in order to flee the banality of our obsequious and conforming lives. These desires, I see Eastwood arguing in *Unforgiven*, are more complicated than they may seem, and our real desires may not be as we think they are.

Metaphysical Levels of Misé en Scene; Metaphysical Levels of Reality

Unforgiven begins with a complicated series of cuts that suggest multiple narrative levels and even multiple metaphysical levels. The opening shot is of a house, a man, and a tree just after sunset. The house, man, and tree are seen in silhouette as they are backlit by the orange of fading day. The man has finished the work of filling in a grave, the grave of his dead wife. We know it is his dead wife because accompanying this image is a text that explains who this man is, who his wife was, and what happened to her. The text provides particulars to the silhouetted forms and what happened to her. The text provides particulars to the silhouetted forms that the image alone does not provide. As silhouetted forms, without particular characteristics identifiable, the image suggests that these are primordial, universal forms, the frontier house, Yggdrasil the Norse Tree of Life, Man, in his primordial, universal activity, burying a loved one.

Just this opening shot implies multiple levels of reality. *Misé en scene* refers to anything that is 'put' in the scene. In this case, the misé en scene includes both the text and the silhouetted figures of man, tree, and house, which imply at least two levels of reality. There is the reality of the man at work burying his dead wife. There is the reality of the text on the screen. And there is also the reality suggested by the point of view of the camera, a point of view bearing witness to this painful scene, which then points to still another reality beyond the reality of the framed shot because we, as the audience, share this point of view, and this act of bearing witness.

The ambiguity of the opening shot compels the audience to interpret it, which is to compel the audience to reflect or think, which is what it means to do philosophy. I take it that part of what *Unforgiven* is about is a reflection on the nature of what it means to be a human being, and perhaps more specifically, even though there are some very strong women characters in the film, what it means to be a man. Some of the issues the movie addresses have to do with what love means, what friendship means, what loyalty and duty mean, what family means, and what life means. These are deep philosophical issues and each of the characters in the movie will encounter these issues in different ways and arrive at different solutions to the problems these issues pose. It is not clear to me that the movie itself proposes a preferred solution for the life issues it addresses so much as it suggests the tragic inadequacy of all attempts to resolve these issues in a fully satisfactory way.

The second shot of the movie is another long shot, also beautiful, but beautiful in a very different way from the first shot. Whereas the first shot is beautiful as elegiac composition, the second shot is beautiful as Sublime Nature: a powerful thunderstorm in some distant mountains descending on a small, vulnerable looking town. Again, the scene contains text that gives particulars to this universal (universal in the sense of archetypal) image of raw nature: "Big Whisky, Wyoming 1880." The music has been replaced with the sound of the distant thunder. The next shot is an almost claustrophobic shot, at night, of the main street of a very small pioneer town in pounding rain. The empty street is lit by light from the building windows, but that light ends in an opaque blackness where the streets head out of town into the night. This shot will be repeated near the end of the movie when William Munny (Clint Eastwood) returns for his vengeance. This shot is followed by a weird dream-like panning shot across the rain-drenched outside of a building, picking up strange shadows acting out uninterpretable scenes behind shaded windows. This dream-like ambiguity is resolved in the next shot of a man vigorously sexually riding a woman in a bed. She is urging him on. From the next room comes a cry, the man's buddy calling for him. The man runs to his buddy's aid in the next room, and there we see the other man attacking a young woman, another prostitute, with a knife, slashing her face, screaming violent things at her. The knife is very large, compensation, no doubt, for what we will learn is his surprisingly small penis. Knives and guns are always compensations for our inadequacies, which is not to say that they are not also extremely useful tools. The philosophical point is to remember that both are true.

Freud's Primal Scene and Philosophy

These scenes near the beginning of *Unforgiven* of shadows moving behind screened windows, shadows of people performing some kind of weird, eerie movements that we, the audience, do not know quite how to interpret, but which seem vaguely disturbing, invoke Freud's idea of the Primal Scene. The Primal Scene, according to Freud, occurs when a young child happens to witness his or her parents making love.[189] The child, according to Freud, cannot tell if this is a scene of violence or affection. What makes it primal is that the child is compelled, due to the intense nature of the scene, to form an interpretation of what is going on before he or she has any conceptual tools for really understanding what is going on. In this way, Freud's Primal Scene stands as well for the primal scene of philosophy. Philosophy is all about trying to understand what we do not understand, trying to invent conceptual tools to understand something we have no conceptual tools for understanding. A version of the Primal Scene (perhaps not quite as Freud meant it) is, therefore, recapitulated every time one finds oneself in a situation in which one can recognize that there is more going on than one can understand, especially if what is going on has overtones of violence, or sex, or both. Many good movies put us into this position at their outset, in the position of sensing that there is something important going on, something to do with violence or sex, but we cannot tell quite what it is.

Slavoj Žižek has argued that this is a repeated trope in the films of Hitchcock, for example. In Hitchcock, the representation of the Primal Scene repeatedly takes a very similar form: we, the audience, as well as some of the characters in the movie, will see a couple in the distance, usually on some kind of hillock, engaged in some kind of intense communication, and we cannot be sure whether it is a violent argument or an intense declaration of love.[190] We are forced, given the intensity of the scene, to try to interpret what it means without sufficient information to make a reliable interpretation. This is what Eastwood is doing at the beginning of *Unforgiven*. Intentionally or not, the dream-like quality of the images that do not seem to make any sense, recapitulates for us the sense of the Primal Scene, of bearing witness to something of evident importance that we do not have the resources to parse and understand. That it is intentional is certainly suggested when the shadows we see through the window get translated into a man having vigorous, if not violent, sex with a woman (which is the Primal Scene just as Freud described it, although not including the detail of a *tergo*), and then the connection with actual violence is made explicit via a montage from that scene of sex to the next scene of the cowboy yelling at the young prostitute and then cutting her face.

What Eastwood is doing here is a form of philosophy done with images instead of words. Hitchcock called this "pure cinema,"[191] when concepts are generated by means of linked images, or montage. The concepts generated by Eastwood in this opening sequence have to do with the human condition, which is what makes them philosophical. We all live with the specter of death in the background. We all live with raw nature towering above us, and working inside us to challenge our civilized veneer. We all repeatedly recapitulate the basic pattern of the Primal Scene, the experience of finding ourselves in situations beyond our understanding, especially situations that involve sex and violence, where we have to try to interpret what is going on without sufficient conceptual tools. Philosophy is about trying to come up with some better conceptual tools for dealing with our lives.

Eastwood and the Western

Eastwood is a master of the Western, both as an actor and as a director. The genre of the Western invokes mythic themes: good versus evil, civilization versus barbarity, man versus nature. The hero, therefore, must be a superior, or, at least, a different sort of person. As an actor, Eastwood did this in the spaghetti Westerns with Sergio Leone through a combination of minimal talk and a maximum of gun fighting skill—these combined with an ironic detachment that made him seem to be concerned with other-worldly things even as he obsessively pursued this world's riches. As a director, he does it in movie after movie through various narrative techniques, such as giving his protagonists a mysterious past or just an inner commitment that is different from and unknown to the rest of the people that surround him. His characters are both subject to fate, they endure terrible beatings, hardships, and cruelties; and superior to fate, they emerge from all hardships somehow essentially unscathed, as if they had some secret connection with the realm of the immortals.[192] His protagonists have a dignity that manifests itself not continually but in moments. It shines through the worst degradations of dirt and violence. We see in these moments a glimpse of something redemptive. In *Unforgiven*, these moments are especially striking because the character of William Munny is so generally unpleasant, unattractive, and unheroic.

Consider a couple of such moments from one of Eastwood's early movies directed by Sergio Leone. In *The Good, the Bad, and the Ugly* (1966) there are two moments of this kind of redemptive dignity that are especially striking. One is when Tucco (Eli Wallach) and Blondie (Clint Eastwood), in an uneasy truce, are trying to find the graveyard where the money for which they are searching is buried. They come across a drunken Union general (Aldo Giuffrè) who has orders to take a particular bridge. The opposing Confederate general clearly has the same orders. Each day both sides attack, meeting at the bridge. Many men are killed and wounded pointlessly, and no progress is made by either side. In a very uncharacteristically selfless gesture, Tucco and Blondie decide to blow up the bridge. It is the last thing that the now wounded and dying general sees, the end of this pointless waste of mens' lives in the exploding bridge. These two Bad Men, Bad Men in the sense that they live outside the law, perform a supremely moral act, an act that the system of law itself cannot accomplish—the end of the senseless killing of hundreds of men

Another moment of surprising redemptive poignancy is when Tucco and Blondie are at the monastery where Tucco's brother, Father Pablo Ramirez (Luigi Pistilli), is a monk. There is a tense scene between Tucco and his brother. It is a scene that is meant to be in private, but Blondie bears witness to the scene through a doorway. In the scene, Tucco's brother tells Tucco of the death of their mother, and then viciously denounces Tucco. Tucco is clearly hurt by these accusations, but when he comes out, he tells Blondie how much his brother loves him. Blondie just says, "Yeah," but as they are riding away on a buckboard, Blondie hands Tucco his cigar for a puff, a gesture of solidarity between unloved outcasts, and a silent affirmation that, in this world, the good are not always so good, and the bad may have some good in them yet.

In *Unforgiven*, three such moments can be identified. One moment is the complicated scene in which the two cowboys, Quick Mike (David Mucci) and Davey Bunting (Rob Campbell), return to town with the horses for the owner of the whore house, Skinny Dubois (Anthony James). One of the cowboys, Davey, the one who did not do the cutting, brings a special horse for the cut prostitute,

Delilah (Anna Levine). There is a moment of temporal suspension when the various moral issues are weighed. On the one hand, the cowboys are honoring their promise and even going beyond what they promised in an attempt at restitution. They are doing something 'good'. On the other hand, the very act of restitution seems to affirm the commodity status of the women, that justice for them can be achieved via a commodity exchange. But the cowboys also bring a gift, an additional horse, for the woman who was cut, which would seem to transcend the mere exchange of commodities. Delilah, the cut prostitute, her face healing, seems to respond positively to this offer of a gift, as do we, the audience, but the woman who is leading the demands for justice for the prostitutes, Strawberry Alice (Francis Fisher), refuses the horse. It is a complicated moment because all of the various claims—moral, practical, political—are brought into salience. We feel and see the rightness of Strawberry Alice's insistence on the insufficiency of this gesture by the cowboys for rectifying the terrible injustice that has been done, and we feel the strong desire for this gift to be accepted and the hope that all can move forward and escape the terrible logic of strict justice via vengeance. We feel the need and desire of the cowboys to try to do something to rectify the injustice that has been done. We see the desire in Delilah to be able to just accept the horse, to be just a regular person again instead of the center of a cause, to begin to put the whole thing behind her. We see Skinny, in some sense, the real source of the deepest forms of the injustice that has been committed, by his demand for financial restitution for the damaging of his 'property,' watching, more or less indifferent to the issues raised by this gesture refused. It is a scene of great and ambiguous moral complexity that emerges from what would seem to be a straightforward exchange. The multiplicity of perspectives that the scene engages reflects a multiplicity of narratives present simultaneously.

Another scene of subtly rendered moral complexity would be Munny's surprising reflection on what it means to kill a man, "It's a hell of a thing, killing a man. Take away all he's got and all he's ever gonna have." The Schofield Kid (Jaime Wentz) says, "Yeah, well, I guess they had it coming." Munny replies, "We all got it coming, kid." This is surprising because up to this point Munny has been as verbally unreflective as he has been inept with a gun or a horse. This display of depth, his sympathy for the killed and his sense of justice, suggest aspects of his character that we had not expected.

A final example is the scene between Munny and Delilah, in which Munny speaks movingly of his wife and, when offered "a free one" (i.e., sex with no charge) from Delilah, Munny refuses the offer. Delilah is clearly hurt by his refusal. She seems to understand it as a rejection of her offer because of her disfigurement, that Munny thinks she is too ugly to have sex with. Munny sees her hurt response and says, "You ain't ugly like me. It's just that we both got scars. But you're a beautiful woman and if I was to want a free one, I'd want it with you. I guess, more than with them other two. It's that I can't on account of my wife." It is a touching scene because Delilah is trying to do something nice for Munny and Munny is trying to do something nice for Delilah. It is a scene of remarkable tenderness within a movie of remarkable violence. The scene humanizes them both, revealing still more layers of moral and human complexity. Again, our expectations are upended, our ability to read a person's character is called into question, we are confronted with the fact that we may not really know what we think we know. We realize that things are more complicated than they initially appeared. This is perhaps the most fundamental philosophical realization.

Wilderness and Civilization

A recurrent theme in the genre of the Western film, and especially in the Westerns of John Ford (e.g., *The Man Who Shot Liberty Valance*), but also a the theme of Sergio Leone's *Once Upon a Time in the West*, is the theme of historical transition from a time when wilderness and wildness dominate to a time when civilization and order dominate (usually marked in Westerns by the construction of tracks for, or the arrival of, a train). There is a macrocosm/microcosm corollary that is also a part of this historical transition in that, just as a society must become more ordered and law-bound, so too must the individuals within that society. As the society becomes more civilized, the society's heroes will be more civilized. They will be bringers of civilization rather than wildness. An individual with self-control and a society under the rule of law makes possible a stable, well-ordered, bourgeois life. This is a great gain. What is lost is the intensity, the spontaneity, the deep satisfaction of doing what one wants, of being the source of the law as opposed to being subject to law. Stability and order are gained, but at the price of meekness, docility, and cooperativeness.

At the beginning of the movie, Munny has given up drinking and violence for a life as a pig farmer, a life that is more stable, well-ordered, and with the potential for a lasting happiness. He has married, had children, acquired a farm—all of these require more and more self-control in turn. All of these require a suppression of one's inner wildness, and Munny had been, by all accounts, exceptionally wild, but, as he says to Ned (Morgan Freeman), "I'm not like that anymore. I'm just like anybody else."

For Munny, however, this life of being the same as everyone else is not going so well. His wife dies, the pig farming is a struggle, and the future for his children is very uncertain. Then an opportunity appears in the form of the Schofield Kid, an opportunity to make a substantial amount of money for something that he used to do for free. At first he resists the offer, but finding himself face down in pig shit he reconsiders. His pigs, his shit, and that is where civil society leaves most of us, deep in our own shit. That is, for the great benefits of living in a civilized society, we must repress, as Freud says, our wildness. We cannot discharge our anger freely when we feel anger. We cannot act on our lusts freely when we feel lust. We cannot act on our impulses to violence when we feel the impulse to commit violence. On the one hand, thank God that we do not, and others do not as well. On the other hand, the suppression of all of those impulses does not make those impulses go away. They accrue and become a kind a sty in which we wallow.

Westerns represent a kind of dream of freedom from all of those repressions civil society demands of us. In Westerns, men are wild, one with nature, out in nature; they fight when they are angry, they fight when they are happy, they pursue the woman they desire without equivocation or art. The 'bad' men are frightening, but also fascinating. Even the 'good' men, tend to be liminal figures in

Westerns, halfway between the wildness of the bad and the tameness of the good. They have some self-control, some sense of deference to law, but are also quick to and able at violence if the situation calls for it. John Ford's Westerns contain many examples of such figures: Tom Doniphon (John Wayne) in *The Man Who Shot Liberty Valance* (1962), Ethan Edwards (John Wayne) in *The Searchers* (1956), Wyatt Earp (Henry Fonda) in *My Darling Clementine* (1946). These films explicitly mark the transition in societies from pre-civilized, pre-law ruled to societies civilized and under the rule of law. The times are thrilling in the pre-law, pre-civilization portion of the films, and wistful in the sequences when the transition has been made. Ford does not seem to be saying in these films that lawlessness is better than law, but only that something is lost when law and civilization are fully instantiated. The question, then, is what do we really want? Do we really want the order and banality of civilized society, or do we really want the wildness that is displayed in the figure of the Westerner, the power of the gun, the closeness to wild nature? The wildness of the Westerner is a kind of play, but it is play for mortal stakes.

Bad Men at Play

You don't know how to play...
            – Cheyenne (Jason Robards) in Leone's *Once Upon a Time in the West*

There are several references to Bad Men as a specific type in *Unforgiven*. Little Bill (Gene Hackman) explicitly denies that the cowboys who were involved in the cutting of the prostitute Delilah are Bad Men. When he is considering what the appropriate justice is for the cutting of a whore, he considers whipping, but settles finally on a fine – five ponies from one of the cowboys and two from the other. Alice is aghast and says, "It ain't fair Little Bill. It ain't fair." Little Bill takes her aside and says, "Haven't you seen enough blood for one night, huh? Hell Alice, it ain't like they was tramps or loafers or Bad Men..." When Will Munny goes to his friend Ned Logan to have him ride with him and the Schofield Kid to kill the cowboys and get the reward, Ned says to him, "Hell, Will. We ain't Bad

Men no more. Shit, we're farmers." Little Bill is a Bad Man still, and so is English Bob, though not quite so Bad as Little Bill. And Little Bill has got nothing on Will Munny when he returns to his Bad Man ways. The Schofield Kid thinks he wants to be a Bad Man, but he will change his mind once he has a taste of what it really means to be a Bad Man.

The theme of many classic Westerns is that of Bad Men at play. Johan Huizinga, in his book, *Homo Ludens*, suggests that along with *Homo Faber*, Man the Maker, and *Homo Sapiens*, Man the Knower, we should be known as *Homo Ludens*, Man the Player. Huizinga's book is a sustained argument for the idea that there is an element of play in all manifestations of culture, that "culture itself bears the character of play."[193] Much of culture, especially under capitalism, will seem to be anti-play, to be about profit, not play. This is the version of capitalism as an expression of the Protestant work ethic, and the early influences of Puritanism in the founding of America, which is also a Christianizing of America.[194] Huizinga equates play with freedom: "Here, then, we find the first main characteristic of play: that it is free, is in fact freedom."[195] Where society oppresses and forces us to repress, play is the release from oppression and repression. We are fascinated with Bad Men, in part, because they live for a particular kind of play that most of us cannot afford to engage in, and, in that pursuit, are free in a way most of us are not.

Sergio Leone, to whom (along with Don Siegal) *Unforgiven* is dedicated, was the master of the Bad Men at play theme. In *The Good, the Bad, and the Ugly*, the gold the three men are looking for is a McGuffin. None of them cares about the gold. What would they do with it if they got it? Open a nice little dry goods store? The gold is just an opportunity for the Bad Men to play together. It is just the flag in a game of 'capture the flag.' The fun is getting it, and winning the game. It is in competing with the other Bad Men for it. There are some minimal rules to the game, but the game itself is outside societal laws and concerns. The only thing the three Bad Men really care about is each other.

The philosophy of Bad Men is best articulated in Leone's *Once Upon a Time in the West* (1968), a film that Sergio Leone originally offered to Clint Eastwood (as the Harmonica character), but which Eastwood decided not to do.[196] In a crucial scene that introduces the character Cheyenne, and shows the initial encounter between Cheyenne and Harmonica (a scene which immediately follows a scene that is beautifully done, in which Cheyenne escapes from the law officers transferring him to a new prison—an escape we hear but do not see; we see only the response of the bar keeper, as he waits to see who will come through the swinging doors of the bar) we get the preliminary formulation of this philosophy. It is Cheyenne who walks through the swinging doors, his hands still shackled, acting the role of the Bad Man. "Whiskey," is his first word. After a drink of whiskey, he looks around at the other people in the bar, sizing them up. At one point one of the men in the saloon, who is seated and in the somewhat dandified dress of a gambler, slowly starts to reach for his pistol. Cheyenne spots it and only wags his finger at him. "Tch, tch, tch" he says, "You don't know how to play." The man, acknowledging this truth, returns his gun to his holster. Cheyenne, as if to prove his point, instructs the man to pull his gun, holding out his manacled hands. As the man draws his gun, Cheyenne aims his own gun at the man's head. He says to the man, "Shoot." The man shoots the manacles, freeing Cheyenne's hands. Just at that moment we hear the haunting sound of a harmonica from some unseen source. Cheyenne goes over to a dark corner from where the harmonica sound seems to be coming. A man sits in the shadows, playing. Cheyenne slides over a light hooked on a line to reveal Harmonica (Charles Bronson). Harmonica's playing is an announcement that he knows how to play. Cheyenne tries to intimidate him, but Harmonica cannot be intimidated. Cheyenne can see it right away, that this is also a real Bad Man. The ground rules for Bad Men play are shown, not said: You must be completely confident in your skill with a gun. You must be willing to kill. Finally, you must be willing to die.

The culmination of the Bad Men at play philosophy is most fully articulated by Frank (Henry Fonda) near the very end of *Once Upon a Time in the West*. Frank is a very Bad Man, but he knows himself and he knows Bad Men and he will give the best account of how a bad man thinks. Leading up to the final confrontation of the film, Harmonica is sitting on a fence whittling, waiting for something, or someone. When Jill (Claudia Cardinale) asks Cheyenne, "Cheyenne, what's he waiting for out there? What's he doing?" Cheyenne answers, "He's whittlin' on a piece of wood. I got a feelin' when he stops whittlin', something's gonna happen." Frank rides up through a hoard of men working on laying railroad tracks (civilization is coming, but it is not there yet) and dust flying. It is a classic shot, contrasting the past, Frank, with the future, the multicultural mix of men working on the railroad, the machine line that will literally bring the future to the West. Frank is steering straight for Harmonica. Harmonica has his gun propped on the fence post in front of him, not threateningly, but as an obvious precaution for dealing with a man like Frank. When Frank rides up to him they have the following conversation:

Frank: "Surprised to see me?"
Harmonica: "I knew you'd come."

(Frank dismounts from his horse, slowly, carefully, keeping his eyes on Harmonica.)

Frank: "Morton once told me I could never be like him. Now I understand why. It wouldn'ta bothered him knowing you were around somewhere alive."
Harmonica: "So, you found out you're not a business man after all."
Frank: "Just a man."
Harmonica: "An ancient race...."

(Harmonica looks up, wistful, looks off at the railroad workers.)

"...Other mortals'll be along, and they'll kill it off."
Frank: "The future doesn't matter to us. Nothing matters now, not the land, not the money, not the woman. I came to see you, because now I know you'll tell me what you're after."

(Harmonica gets off the fence in the same way that Frank got off his horse, carefully, slowly, eyes on Frank.)

Harmonica: "Only at the point of dying."
Frank: "I know."

Huizinga argues that play is an essential feature of human nature. Capitalism is in its essence anti-play in the way that it makes capital—the idea that everything has a price—the basis of our relationship to the world. Capitalism wants everyone to be a businessman (business person) after all. Bad men preserve the spirit of play. Pure play is inherently pointless. Or rather, it is its own point. For the Bad Man, as Frank says, it's not about the land, not the money, it's not even about the woman, it is about the play. This is play beyond good and evil. When Frank maneuvers to have the sun in Harmonica's eyes for the final showdown, that is not evil, and Harmonica shows no emotion about the development. It is precisely what he expects from Frank. When Cheyenne is trying to explain to Jill about men like them, he says, "You don't understand, Jill. People like that have something inside, something to do with death." It is an obvious statement. On the one hand, since Frank is certainly a killer, and Harmonica kills some men himself, but that obscures the real meaning of the claim. The important way in which men like Frank and Harmonica have something to do with death is that they are not afraid of it. They are not trying to buy or earn their way out of the deal. The games they like to play summon death as a player. Death is explicitly a part of the game they play. There would be no game if death were not present.[197]

The Banality of Goodness, the Goodness of Banality

Slavoj Žižek has written about a secret terror at the heart of the bourgeois, well-socialized, good capitalist life, especially for men. It is the terror of banality. Talking about David Lynch's *Lost Highway* (1997), Žižek contrasts the opposition of two horrors confronting the modern bourgeois man: "the fantasmatic horror of the nightmarish noir universe of perverse sex, betrayal, and murder, and the (perhaps much more unsettling) despair of our drab, 'alienated' daily life of impotence and distrust."[198] The one terror is of falling out of the bourgeois world into a lawless noir world of id. The other terror, the more unsettling, is to maintain one's place in the bourgeois world. The bourgeois capitalist life, for those who can achieve it, is very well protected against the assaults of the world. The price paid for that security is a sense of the absolute banality lurking at the core of that existence. This is what Thoreau described as "lives of quiet desperation."[199] Bad, desperate, men avoid that particular existential night of the soul. There may be other nights of the soul for Bad Men, but not that one.

William Munny has given up his Bad Man ways, and taken on the values of the Christianized morality of his wife for his wife's sake, but also, no doubt, for his own sake. The material counterpart of this soul renunciation is the renunciation of alcohol, which always accompanied his Bad Man play. Throughout *Unforgiven*, Munny is offered many opportunities to take a drink, something he, and everyone else, knows will make what they have to do a lot easier, and in every case he refuses the drink. One plot line this refusal introduces into the narrative of the movie is the question, when will Munny take a drink? What will it take to make him take a drink? Bad Men may not have any sort of morals according to societal standards, but they do have principles that resemble a moral code, each his own, I suppose, but clearly for Munny there is something in his code about honoring men he has ridden with who have proved themselves as worthy to ride with. Munny takes a terrible beating from Little Bill, a beating that almost kills him, but does not turn to drink on that account. Instead, he turns the other cheek and continues to live up to his version of Christian values. When Munny learns that Little Bill has beaten and killed his friend Ned, however, that is another thing altogether. It is time to drink.

Drink releases the Bad Man in Munny, the man secreted inside the man that Munny has tried to make himself into. The ending of the movie begins with a return to the opening shots of the streets of the town of Big Whiskey at night and in the rain. William Munny is riding into town, swigging whiskey all the way. Now it's not about the land or the money, or even the women. He's come to see Little Bill. Now we see what all of those rumors and stories about him are really about. He is a cold blooded killer. He doesn't mind talking about killing things, as he says, "I've killed women and children. Killed just about everything that walks or crawls at one time or another." But what he is here for is actually to do some killing, which he does with much aplomb.

Our reaction to this killing spree by Munny is complex. In a sense, of course, we, the audience, have been wanting him to take a drink, to return to his old ways, to give up this pathetic, incompetent, persona of Christianized 'goodness.'

We have come to see a Western, for heaven's sakes. On the other hand, just as the earlier, poorly executed killings were painful to watch because they were so inept, these killings are terrifying to watch because they are so ruthlessly efficient. When his gun misfires, Munny does not miss a beat. He proceeds with the next step in killing everyone in the place as though it were obvious and easy. The innocent, if there are any, and the guilty alike, are shot. When Little Bill says, "I don't deserve to die like this." Munny replies, "Deserve's got nothin' to do with it." And that is a terrifying possibility. If our death has nothing to do with deserts, then that raises the question of our lives as well. God insures deserts. It is a godless world in which "deserve's go nothin' to do with it." That is not what we want, to be confronted with the possibility of the meaninglessness of our death, the possibility of the meaninglessness of our life. Eastwood begins by giving us what we think we want, mete and proper vengeance for wrongs done. He ends by confronting us with our worst fears about the possibility of meaning in our lives, which it is the role of philosophy to consider.

It is a hard life being a Bad Man. It may have its joys and intensities, but the price is extremely high—no real friends, no wife, no children, no love, no community. The most you might get, if you are lucky, is someone you ride with about whom you have no complaints. Munny and Ned both gave it up. When we see Munny revert to his Bad Man ways, which is what we want to see, we are horrified by what we see, and by our own desires to see them. What nags at us throughout the movie is the banality of Munny's barely sustained goodness. What we long for is the Bad Man to emerge. When the Bad Man does emerge, we are reminded of what it really means to be a Bad Man, what it really looks like and what the costs are. The message of the film, I think, is that there is no living without a remainder of dissatisfaction. Goodness, being law-abiding, will cost us a certain intensity and freedom in our lives, but get us love, a family, some partial security against the travails of the world. Being a Bad Man may sound like fun, but the costs are extremely high, and there is always a badder man out there, as Little Bill discovered. Good may be banal, but badness is downright terrifying.[200]

Conclusions

Derrida, in "The Law of Genre," connects the concept of genre with its root in the Greek genos which he associates with birth, generous, engendering, genealogy, as well as with genre.[201] Just as noir and westerns are genres of film, philosophy can be understood as a genre of thought. It is a genre of thought that is especially generative, and what it engenders are ideas. Philosophy is committed to the proliferation of ideas. Plato, via Socrates, constructs a case in the *Symposium* for the idea that the ultimate goal for human beings is to reproduce ourselves, and the ultimate form of reproduction is not of things (people), but of ideas, especially beautiful ideas. This is part of his "ladder" of love, which involves an ascension from lower forms of love—the sexual love of bodies--to the highest form of love, which is the reproduction of ideas in beauty.[202]

The directors of the movies that I have been considering in this work—the Coens, Polanski, Scorsese, Lee, Eyre, and Eastwood—are all *auteurs*, which means that they are directors that make movies that are closer to art than they are to just popular entertainment, and their movies reflect a distinctive style so that, once you are familiar with the work of one of these directors, you will be able to recognize their work in the future. Even when they work in a genre, they work at the very edge of the genre boundary, which is the area of maximum ambiguity and fecundity for producing new ideas. In this way, movies function in a way that is very similar to philosophy. They give us new ideas and get us to see things in new ways. The Coens do this with their irony laden perspective. Polanski has a certain European, existential way of seeing that pervades his films. Scorsese is tapped into the dark side of inner city life. Spike Lee opens up the world of what it means to be a black man in a white-dominated world. Chris Eyre lets us, who are not tribal, see inside the lives and worlds of tribal and Native American ways of being in the world. Clint Eastwood returns again and again to the problematic of violence in America, where violence has been so much a source of American identity, but also a source of American despair.

Ideas themselves are prolific. New ideas couple with our established ideas to generate more new ideas. We become new and larger people as we acquire and produce more new ideas. Ideas are like tools, and the more one has, the more new situations one can negotiate. It is not the one with the most toys that wins, or even the one with the most money. It is the one with the most ideas that is the most fully human, the one who has maximized their potential to be human and to understand other human beings.

Postmodernism may be about deconstruction, but every deconstruction generates a reconstruction. Old ideas need to be problematized in order to make space for new ideas. Every creative act requires a certain "incredulity toward metanarratives." The law of genre is the law of the world. Everything is what it is and is not what it is, in the constant evolution of the world, and we need to understand how both are true.

I was standing in line at the bar at a philosophy conference one time. I was behind two men who were talking. One of the men was saying, "I was at an MLA conference a couple of months ago. The thing that was going on was that everyone was trying to sleep with everyone else. At philosophy conferences, everyone just wants to talk and to argue." I don't know if this is true, but there is some truth in it. It is a very Platonic conception of philosophy, the triumph of the mind over the body as expressed in conversation.

Great movies always have more going on in them than we are aware of on a single viewing, just as people are always way more complicated than we can ever discern on a single encounter. Movies, like people, take time to unpack, to learn their secrets, to learn their secret wisdom. What we learn will be about the ideas they generate. In this work I have tried to unpack some of the ideas produced by some great auteur directors in some exceptional examples of their work. These works of art have produced some new ideas for me, and I have tried to pass these ideas on to others. What is most beautiful may not be the ideas themselves so much as the process that occurs when we try to share ideas with each other in conversations. My hope is that these essays on these movies will produce some new ideas for others, but even more deeply I hope that the ideas will generate topics for conversations, in which even more new ideas are produced.

That would represent Plato's highest wish for us, that we reproduce new ideas in beauty, the beauty of a philosophical conversation.

Notes

Introduction

1. Jean-François Lyotard, *The Postmodern Condition: A Report on Knowledge*, translated by Geoff Bennington and Brian Massumi (Minneapolis: University of Minnesota Press, 1979), xxiv.
2. Jacque Derrida, "The Law of Genre," *Critical Inquiry*, Vol. 7, No. 1. On Narrative (Autumn, 1980), 58.
3. Derrida says, "…from one repetition to the next, a change had insinuated itself into the relationship between the two initial utterances." "The Law of Genre," 58.
4. *Ibid.*, 57.
5. *Ibid.*
6. Bertrand Russell, "Vagueness," originally printed in *Australian Journal of Philosophy and Psychology* 1 (1923). Reprinted in *Vagueness*: A Reader, edited by Rosanna Keefe and Peter Smith (Cambridge: The MIT Press, 1997), 63.
7. Peter Unger, "Skepticism and Nihilism," *Nous*, vol. 14, No. 4 (Nov. 1980), 519-20.
8. Stanley Fish, Surprised by Sin: The Reader in Paradise Lost (Berkeley: University of California Press, 1971), 1.
9. "The Law of Genre," 59.
10. Ibid.
11. Plato, *Symposium*, translated by Alexander Nehemas & Paul Woodruff (Indianapolis: Hackett, 1989), 77 (223D, 4-8).

1 | *Raising Arizona* as an American Comedy and as a Comedy about America

12. Peter Körte and Georg Seesslen, editors, *Joel & Ethan Coen* (New York: Procenium Publishers, Inc., 2001), 172.
13. Ralph Waldo Emerson, "The Transcendentalist" in *The Portable Emerson*, edited by Carl Bode in collaboration with Malcolm Cowley (New York: Penquin Books, 1981), 99.
14. Joel Coen & Ethan Coen, *Raising Arizona: The Screenplay* (New York: St. Martin's Press, 1988), viii.
15. See the Smithsonian Folkways Recordings song list for the album *Darling Corey and Goofing Off Suite* by Pete Seeger (1993), catalogue # 40018 at www.Folkways.si.edu. Raising Arizona, 5.
16. *Raising Arizona*, 5.
17. See Robert Frost's poem "Two Tramps in Mud Time or, A Full-Time Interest" in *Robert Frost: Collected Poetry, Prose, and Plays* (Library of America, 1995), 251.
18. John Winthrop, "A Model of Christian Charity," delivered in 1630. Available online at: http://winthropsociety.com/doc_charity.php.

19. In the original VHS format the title had a colon followed by the phrase "An Unbelievable Comedy."
20. Aristotle, *Poetics I*, translated by Richard Janko (Indianapolis: Hackett Publishing Company, Inc., 1987)
21. Dante's own title was (in translation): "Begins the Comedy of Dante Alighieri, Flornetine in Birth, Not in Custom." "The Divine" was added later. A translation of Dante's letter to Can Grande can be found on the web at http://ccat.sas.upenn.edu/jod.cangrande.english.html.
22. This is what Jean Paul Sartre calls "*mauvais foi*" or "bad faith."
23. *Raising Arizona*, 9.
24. Martin Heidegger, *Being and Time*, translated by John Macquarrie & Edward Robinson (New York: Harper & Row, Publishers, 1962), 328.
25. Alain Badiou, Ethics: *An Essay on the Understanding of Evil*, translated by Peter Hallward (New York: Verso, 2002), 67-69.
26. Alain Badiou, *Infinite Thought: Truth and the Return to Philosophy*, translated by Oliver Feltham and Justin Clemens (New York: Continuum, 2004), 52.
27. *Raising Arizona*, 16.
28. Georg Seesslen, "Looking for a Trail in Coen County" in *Joe & Ethan Coen*, 230, 277.
29. Plato, *Republic*, translated by G. M.A. Grube, revised by C. D. C. Reeve (Indianapolis: Hackett Publishing Company, Inc., 1992), Bk. VII, lines 516e-518c.
30. Ted Cohen, *Jokes: Philosophical Thoughts on Joking Matters* (Chicago: The University of Chicago Press, 1999), 10.
31. *Jokes*, 25.
32. Dante Alighieri, *The Inferno*, translated by John Ciardi (New York: New American Library, 1954), 28.
33. R. Barton Palmer, *Joel and Ethan Coen* (Urbana: University of Illinois Press, 2004), 129.
34. Friedrich Nietzsche, *Human, All too Human: A Book for Free Spirits*, translated by Marion Faber (Lincoln: University of Nebraska Press, 1986), §5. That section begins, "In ages of crude, primordial cultures, man thought he could come to know a second real world in dreams: this is the origin of all metaphysics."
35. Delmore Schwartz, *In Dreams Begin Responsibilities and Other Stories* (New York: New Directions Publishing Corporation, 1978).
36. *Raising Arizona*, 41.
37. The original essay, entitled "Pictures That Do the Talking," is from 2001 and is reprinted in William Rodney Allen, editor, *The Coen Brothers: Interviews* (Jackson: University Press of Mississippi, 2006), 158.
38. *The Coen Brothers: Interviews*, 157.
39. *Raising Arizona*, 22.
40. *Ibid.*, 53.

2 | *No Country for Old Men*: The Coens' Tragic Western

41. I am citing dialogue from the movie based on a combination of my memory and on a script posted on the internet at:
http://www.youknowforkids.com/nocountryforoldmen.txt, 90.
42. From an online script at:
http://www.weeklyscript.com/O%20Brother%20Where%20Art%20Thou.txt.
43. Henry James, "The Art of Fiction," at:
http://guweb2.gonzaga.edu/faculty/campbell/engl462/artfiction.html.
44. Jacques Derrida, "The Law of Genre," Glyph 7 (1980), 206.
45. Cormac McCarthy, *No Country for Old Men* (New York: Vantage Books, 2005).
46. Script, 8.
47. I have in mind the following sentences from "The American Scholar": "The state of society is one in which the members have suffered amputation form the trunk, and strut about so many walking monsters—a good finger, a neck, a stomach, an elbow, but never a man….In this view of him, as Man Thinking, the theory of his office is contained. Him Nature solicits with all her placid, all her monitory pictures…." Ralph Waldo Emerson, Ralph Waldo Emerson: Essays & Lectures (New York: The Library of America, 1983), 54.
48. Aristotle, *Nicomachean Ethics*, translated by Martin Oswald (New York: Macmillan Publishing Company, 1962), 1123b.
49. Heraclitus, in *The Presocratics*, edited by Philip Wheelwright (New York: Macmillan Publishing Company, 1966), 71 (fragments 91-2).
50. Ibid., 78 (fragment 79).
51. Hermann Fränkel, "A Thought Pattern in Heraclitus," in *The Pre-Socratics: A Collection of Essays*, edited by Alexander P. D. Mourelatos (Princeton: Princeton University Press, 1974), 214.
52. Script, 4-5. It is worth noting that this is pure Coen brothers. This parallel between Chigurh and Moss is not made explicit in the book in the same way. In the book, Chigurh says to the man, "Would you step away from the car please." McCarthy adds the detail, "He placed his hand on the man's head like a faith healer" just before Chigurh pops him in the forehead with the cattle stun gun.
53. Script, 85-6.
54. *Nicomachean Ethics*, Book Nine, 1166a29.
55. "There is but one truly serious philosophical problem, and that is suicide. Judging whether life is or is not worth living amounts to answering the fundamental question of philosophy." Albert Camus, "An Absurd Reasoning," *The Myth of Sisyphus*, trans. Justin O'Brien (New York: Vintage, 1955), 3.
56. In the book there is a passage in which Bell reflects on something is father once said to him, "My daddy always told me to just do the best you knew how and to tell the truth. He said there was nothing to set a man's mind at ease like wakin up in the morning

and not havin to decide who you were. And if you done something wrong just stand up and say you done it and say you're sorry and get on with it. Dont haul stuff around with you" (McCarthy, *No Country*, 249). Those same ethical rules are implicit for Bell in the movie as well.

57. Script, 19.
58. McCarthy, *No Country*, 259.
59. Friedrich Nietzsche, *The Birth of Tragedy*, translated by Walter Kaufman (New York: Vantage Books, 1967), see especially §§11-12.
60. Roderick Frazier Nash, *Wilderness and the American Mind* (New Haven: Yale University Press, 1982), 1-2.
61. *Ibid*, xii.
62. *Ibid.*, xiii-xiii.
63. *Ibid.*, 27.
64. Henry David Thoreau, *Walking* (Whitefish, MT: Kessinger Publishing, 2004), Part II, §14.
65. Jane Tompkins, *West of Everything: The Inner Life of Westerns* (New York: Oxford University Press, 1992), 23-67. Peter A. French, *Cowboy Metaphysics: Ethics and Death in Westerns* (New York: Rowman & Littlefield Publishers, Inc., 1997), 1-45.
66. French, 47.
67. Louis L'Amour, *Hondo* (New York: Bantam Books, 1953), 59. Cited in Tompkins, 23.
68. Tompkins, 24.
69. French, 57.
70. Script, 2.
71. McCarthy, *No Country*, 227.
72. *Ibid.*, 267.
73. *Ibid.*, 281.
74. *Ibid.*, 259.
75. Script, 115.
76. A. Weismann, "La durée de la vie," in Essais sur l'hérédité" (Paris: C. Reinwald et Cie, 1892). Quoted in François Jacob, *The Possible and the Actual* (Seattle: University of Washington Press, 1982), 50.
77. Jacob, 51.
78. William Butler Yeats, *The Collected Poems of W. B. Yeats* (New York: Macmillan Publishing Company, 1979), 191.
79. William Butler Yeats, *A Vision* (New York: Collier Books, 1965), 279.
80. Script, 122.

3 | **The Dark Sublimity of *Chinatown***

81. The first articles in French identifying noir as something like a genre were Nino Frank's "Un nouveau genre 'policier': L'aventure criminelle" and Jean-Pierre Chartier's "Les Américains aussi font des films 'noirs'. See the discussion in James Naremore, *More Than Night: Film noir in its Contexts* (Berkeley: University of California Press, 1998), 15.

82. This point is made in several of the seminal essays on film noir, starting with the essay by Raymond Borde and Étienne Chaumeton (1955) "Towards a Definition of Film Noir" (translated from the French by Alain Silver) from the book *Panorama du Film noir Américain* and by Raymond Durgnat (1970) in "Paint it Black: the Family Tree of the Film Noir" and in "Notes on Film Noir" by Paul Schrader (1972). All of these essays can be found in *Film noir Reader*, edited by Alain Silver and James Ursini (New York: Limelight Editions, 1998).

83. This is a claim made by Nicholas Christopher in *Somewhere in the Night: Film Noir and the American City* (New York: Henry Holt and Company, 1997), 241. James Naremore argues a similar case in his contrast of *Chinatown* with *The Long Goodbye* (Robert Altman, 1973). Naremore argues that although *The Long Goodbye* was made a year earlier, it was more a "halucinatory" parody of noir, than a real return to something profoundly noir, as *Chinatown* was. See James Naremore, *More than Night*, 206-07.

84. Fredric Jameson also makes the connection between *Chinatown* and nostalgia, but to a somewhat different end in "Postmodernism and Consumer Society" in *The Cultural Turn: Selected Writings on the Postmodern, 1983-1998* (New York: Verso, 1998), 8-9. He also talks about nostalgia and film in "Film: Nostalgia for the Present" in *Postmodernism, or the Cultural Logic of Late Capitalism* (Durham: Duke University Press, 2001), 279-96.

85. My thanks to Tony McRae for some technical assistance in tracking down the use of blinds in some of the classic *film noirs*. For more on noir see www.film-trip.com.

86. Paul Ricoeur, *Freud and Philosophy: An Essay on Interpretation* (New Haven: Yale University Press, 1970), 32-33.

87. Ricoeur, 32.

88. T. S. Elliot, the "Burnt Norton" section of *Four Quartets in Collected Poems 1909-1962* (New York: Harcourt, Brace & World, Inc., 1970), 176.

89. Some of the neo-noir twists in *Chinatown* include explicit references to the first classic noir, *The Maltese Falcon*. The whole opening sequence can be read, and has been by several commentators on the film, as a reference to the opening of *The Maltese Falcon*: a woman comes to a detective's office with a bogus story to get him involved in a very complicated plot for her own personal reasons, etc. There is also an explicit reference to the scene of scraping Miles Archer's name off the door with a similar scene in *Chinatown* in which Hollis Mulwray's name is being scraped off a door. A nice Ozymandia-ish comment on the briefness of our tenure on earth. There is also, most strikingly, the appearance of the director of *The Maltese Falcon* in *Chinatown*, John

Huston as the anti-Biblical Noah Cross. For more on the reference to *The Maltese Falcon* in *Chinatown*, see the discussion in *Somewhere in the Night*, 242; and *More than Night*, 207-08.

90. For more on labyrinths in noir, see J. J. Abram's essay, "From Sherlock Holmes to the Hard-Boiled Detective in Film Noir" in *The Philosophy of Film Noir*, ed. Mark T. Conard, University Press of Kentucky, 2005.

91. Daniel C. Dennett, *Conciousness Explained* (Boston: Little, Brown and Company, 1991),324-25.

92. This has frequently been remarked on. Some very good essays on the relationships between the two are: John Bolton, "Language, Oedipus, and *Chinatown*," in MLN, Vol. 106, No. 5, Comparative Literature (Dec., 1991), 933-950; Vernon Shetley, "Incest and Capital in Chinatown," *MLN* Vol. 114, No. 5 (1999), 1092-1109; this connection is alsomade in Michael Eton's BFI book, *Chinatown* (London: BFI Publishing, 1997), 67.

93. This idea is explicitly remarked on by John Bolton in "Language, Oedipus, and Chinatown," 940.

94. A point also made by Eaton, 67.

95. This is a point made by Vernon Shetley, 1094.

96. This line is quoted in one of the earliest and most influential works on *film noir* by Raymond Borde and Étienne Chaumeton entitled *Panorama du Film noir Americin*. They quote this line from a 19th Century pre-surrealist writer Isidore Ducasse, Count Lautréamont. I found it in a excerpted passage: Raymond Borde and Étienne Chaumeton, "Towards a Definition of *Film noir*," translated from the French by Alain Silver, in *Film noir Reader*, 19.

97. Borde and Chaumeton, 25.

98. The classice text on postmodernism, identifying it, naming it, and describing it is Jean-François Lyotard's *The Postmodern Condition* in 1979.

99. Richard Rorty, *The Linguistic Turn: Recent Essays in Philosophical Method* (Chicago: The University of Chicago Press, 1967).

100. Slavoj Žižek, *Looking Awry: An Introduction to Jacques Lacan through Popular Culture* (Cambridge: MIT Press, 1997), 88.

101. Sigmund Freud, *The Uncanny*, translated by David Mclintock (New York: Penguin Books, 2003), 134.

102. Freud, 142.

103. I have in mind here Kant's concept of the sublime. For a more complete explanation see, Immanual Kant, *Critique of Judgement* translated by J. H. Bernard (New York: Prometheus Books, 2000), §§23-29.

104. Aristotle, *Poetics*, translated by Richard Janko (Indianapolis: Hackett Publishing Company, 1987), 7 (49b25).

105. See, for example, James Kavanagh, "*Chinatown*: Other Places, Other Times," in *Jump Cut 3* (1974), 1,8; Andrew Sarris, "*Chinatown* and Polanski-Towne: Tilting toward Tragedy" in *Village Voice* November 7, 1974, 85; Murray Sperber, "'Do As Little As

Possible': Polanski's Message and Manipulation" in *Jump Cut 3* (1974), 9-10.

106. Polanski says this as part of an interview that is provided as additional material on the DVD of the movie *Chinatown*.

4 | Economies of Time in Spike Lee's *Clockers*

107. These shots are recreations of actual police crime photos. As Spike Lee explains, "we reenacted these crime-scene pictures for the opening credits, as we felt it would be disrespectful to the families of the dead to show the real bodies." In, *Spike Lee: That's My Story and I'm Sticking to It*, as told to Kaleem Aftab (New York: W. W. Norton & Company, 2005), 240.

108. *Ibid.*, 4.

109. I am using this term stipulatively, not to designate a racial group, but a social construct. I discuss this idea at further length subsequently.

110. Education & Racism, National Education Association, 1973, 12.

111. Lewis Hyde, *The Gift: Imagination and the Erotic Life of Property* (New York: Random House, 1983), 47.

112. *The Gift*, 33.

113. W. E. B. Du Bois, *The Souls of Black Folk: Essays and Sketches* (New York: Fawcett, 1961, originally published in 1903), 17.

114. James C. McKelly addresses Du Bois's concept of "double consciousness" in Spike Lee's films in his essay "The Double Truth, Ruth: *Do the Right Thing* and the Culture of Ambiguity" in *The Spike Lee Reader*, edited by Paula J. Massood (Philadelphia: Temple University Press, 2007), 58-60.

115. Zora Neale Hurston, *Their Eyes Were Watching God* (New York: J. B. Lippincott Co., 1937), 96. My thanks to Affi Ingberg for this observation.

116. Jean-François Lyotard, *The Postmodern Condition: A Report on Knowledge* (Minneapolis: University of Minnesota Press, 1979), xxiv.

117. Slavoj Žižek, *Organs without Bodies: On Deleuze and Consequences* (New York: Routledge, 2004), 201.

118. *Education & Racism*, 9.

119. As Keith M. Harris puts it, "The housing-project block becomes the slave block..." in his essay "Clockers (Spike Lee, 1995): Adaptation in Black" in *The Spike Lee Reader*, 131.

120. Dan Flory, *Philosophy, Black Film, Film Noir* (University Park: The Pennsylvania State University Press, 2008), 1-2.

121. Richard Rorty, *Contingency, Irony, and Solidarity* (New York: The University of Cambridge Press, 1989), xiv.

122. Paula S. Rothenberg (ed.), *White Privilege: Essential Readings on the Other Side of Racism* (New York: Worth Publishers, 2002). See all four essays in Part Two of this

edited collection. The essays include: James R. Barrett and David Roediger, "How White People Became White"; Karen Brodkin, "How Jews Became White Folks"; Neil Foley, "Becoming Hispanic: Mexican Americans and Whiteness"; and George Lipsitz, "The Possessive Investment of Whiteness."

123. Charles S. Peirce, *The Essential Writings*, edited by Edward C. Moore (New York: Prometheus Books, 1972), 238.

124. This is a different interpretation of this reflection on the surface of the eyeball shot from the one offered by Keith Harris in his essay on *Clockers*, "*Clockers*: Adaptation in Black," in *The Spike Lee Reader*, 131. Harris's interpretation is that we are seeing what Victor is seeing. I cannot disagree with that, but that does not seem to me to be a sufficient explanation for this complex shot.

125. Rosa Parks (with Jim Haskins), *Rosa Parks: My Story* (New York: Dial Books, 1992),116. Rosa Parks makes it very clear that her tiredness is more about having to put up with injustice than it was a physical tiredness: "the only tired I was, was tired of giving in" (116).

126. Cornell West, *Race Matters* (New York: Vintage Books, 1993), 135-36.

127. Peter Unger, *Living High & Letting Die: Our Illusion of Innocence* (New York: Oxford University Press, 1996), 10-11.

128. Peirce, *Essential Writings*, 238.

129. John Dewey, *Art as Experience* (New York: Perigee Books, 1980), 348.

5 | Art, Sex, and Time in Scorsese's *After Hours*

130. Emmanuel Levinas, *Totality and Infinity: An Essay on Exteriority*, translated by Alphonso Lingis (Pittsburgh: Duquesne University Press, 1969), 38.

131. Jean-François Lyotard, *The Postmodern Condition: A Report on Knowledge* translated by Geoff Bennington and Brian Massumi (Minneapolis: University of Minnesota Press, 1984), xxiv.

132. These two quotes from Scorsese are from the voice-over commentary to the DVD. The scene of the keys falling, which includes a shot from the perspective of the keys, was complicated for them to set up, especially with the budget they had. Their first attempt to get it was by tying bungy cords to a camera and throwing it off the roof with Griffin Dunne standing patiently below it. It was so crazily dangerous that they ended up splurging on a crane for the shot.

133. Immanuel Kant, *The Critique of Pure Reason*, translated by Norman Kemp Smith (New York: St. Martin's Press, 1965). Kant's theory of aesthetics is contained in what is known as the third *Critique, The Critique of Judgment*, translated by J. h. Bernard (Amherst, New York: Prometheus Books, 2000).

134. Ludwig Wittgenstein, *Philosophical Investigations*, translated by G. E. M. Anscombe (New York: Macmillan Publishing Company, 1968), Part II, §xi.

135. Immanuel Kant, *Foundations of the Metaphysics of Morals*, translated by Lewis White Beck (New York: Macmillan Publishing Company, 1989), 53 (Akademie edition, 435).

136. Theodor Adorno, *Minima Moralia: Reflections on a Damaged Life*, translated by E. F. N. Jephcott (New York: Verso, 2005), 23.
137. John Dewey, *Art as Experience* (New York: Perigee Books, 1980), 37.
138. *Ibid.*, 36.
139. *Ibid.*, 38.
140. *Ibid.*, 44.
141. *Ibid.*, 40.
142. Michel Chion, *The Voice in Cinema* translated by Claudia Gorbman (New York: Columbia University Press, 1999), especially 17-31.
143. Jean Douchet, "Hitch and His Audience" translated by David Wilson ("Hitch et son Public", *Cahiers du Cinéma* 113, November 1960) in *Cahiers du Cinéma: 1960-1968: New Wave, New Cinema, Reevaluating Hollywood* edited by Jim Hllier (Cambridge: Harvard University Press, 1986), 150-51.
144. Plato, *Phaedrus*, translated by R. Hackworth in *The Collected Dialogues of Plato* edited by Edith Hamilton and Huntington Cairns (Princeton: Princeton University Press, 1961), see, especially 517ff. (Stephanus pagination, 272 ff.).
145. Thomas Nagel, "Sexual Perversion" in *Mortal Questions* (New York: Cambridge University Press, 1979), 44.
146. *Ibid.*, 45. This is the way that Nagel constructs the situation: "Suppose a man and a woman we may call Romeo and Juliet, are at opposite ends of a cocktail lounge, with many mirrors on the walls which permit unobserved observation, and even mutual unobserved observation. Each of them is sipping a martini and studying other people in the mirrors. At some point Romeo notices Juliet. He is moved, somehow, by the softness of her hair and the diffidence with which she sips her martini, and this arouses him sexually…at this stage he is aroused by an unaroused object, so he is more in the sexual grip of his body than of hers. Let us suppose, however, that Juliet now senses Romeo in another mirror on the opposite wall, though neither of them yet knows that he is seen by the other (the mirror angles provide three-quarter views). Romeo then begins to notice in Juliet the subtle signs of sexual arousal, heavy-lidded stare, dilating pupils, faint flush, etc. This of course intensifies her bodily presence…. His arousal is nevertheless still solitary. But now, cleverly calculating the line of her stare without actually looking her in the eyes, he realizes that it is directed at him through the mirror on the opposite wall…. This is definitely a new development, for it gives him a sense of embodiment not only through his own reactions but through the eyes and reactions of another…."
147. Levinas, 39.
148. Mark Taylor, *Altarity* (Chicago: The University of Chicago Press, 1987).
149. This story can be found complete at
www.mala.bc.ca/~johnstoi/kafka/beforethelaw.htm.
150. Slavoj Žižek, *Looking Awry: An Introduction to Jacques Lacan through Popular Culture* (Cambridge: The MIT Press, 1997), 88-91.

151. There are many suggestions in *After Hours* of parallels with Homer's *Odyssey*. Like Odysseus, Paul justs wants to get home. Like Odysseus, Paul encounters a series of very powerful, sometimes dangerous, always challenging women. For Odysseus, these include not just Circe and Calypso, but also the Sirens (who lure men to their death for food), Nausicaa and even the wily Penelope. Odysseus, however, is much better at handling difficult situations than Paul Hackett is.

152. Saint Augustine, Confessions, translated by Henry Chadwick (New York: Oxford University Press, 1992), 230.

153. Michel Foucault, *Discipline and Punish: The Birth of the Prison*, translated by Alan Sheridan (New York: Vantage Books, 1997), 141-162.

154. I heard Mihaly Csikzentmihalyi give the keynote address on "positive psychology" and the idea of "flow" at a SAAP meeting several years ago. He has written several books, including *Flow, The Evolving Self, and Creativity*.

155. Plato, *Phaedrus*, translated by R. Hackworth in *The Collected Dialogues of Plato* edited by Edith Hamilton and Huntington Cairns (Princeton: Princeton University Press, 1961), see, especially 517ff. (Stephanus pagination, 272 ff.).

156. Cynthia Willett in her very interesting essay "Baudrillard, 'After Hours', and the Postmodern Suppression of Socio-Sexual Conflict" in *Cultural Critique*, No. 34 (Autumn, 1996), pp. 143-161 offers a very different reading of the ending of *After Hours* from the one I give here. Her reading is that Paul remains the same at the end, that the movie portrays a kind of postmodern failure of character development.

6 | Regeneration through Stories and Song: The View from the Other Side of the West in Chris Eyre's *Smoke Signals*

157. Richard Slotkin, *Regeneration through Violence: The Mythology of the American Frontier 1600-1860* (Norman: University of Oklahoma Press, 1973), 4.

158. *Regeneration*, 7.

159. Bruce Wilshire, *The Primal Roots of American Philosophy: Pragmatism, Phenomenology, and Native American Thought* (University Park: The Pennsylvania State University Press, 2000), ix.

160. Cornell West, *The American Evasion of Philosophy: A Genealogy of Prgamatism* (Madison: The University of Wisconsin Press, 1989). Stanley Cavell, *The Senses of Walden* (San Fransisco: North Point Press, 1981).

161. Dennis West and Joan M. West, "Sending Cinematic Smoke Signals: An Interview with Sherman Alexie, *Cineaste*, v. 23, n. 4 (Fall, 1998): 28.

162. Screenplay, 9.

163. *Smoke Signals*, 61.

164. Slavoj Žižek, "Alfred Hitchcock, or, The Form and its Historical Mediation" in *Everything You Wanted to Know about Lacan (But Were Afraid to Ask Hitchcock)*, edited by Slavoj Žižek (New York: Verso, 2000), 11n. 3.

165. Slotkin, *Regeneration*, 6.

166. Slotkin, *Regeneration*, 560.

167. Lewis Hyde, *The Gift: Creativity and the Artist in the Modern World* (originally: *The Gift: Imagination and the Erotic Life of Property*) (New York: Vintage Books, 2007), xix.

168. *The Gift*, xxi-xxii.

169. Ibid., 201.

170. *Smoke Signals*, 137.

171. *The Gift*, 4.

172. Ibid., 157.

173. Ibid.,, 22-24.

174. Gregory Cajete, "Philosophy of Native Science" in *American Indian Thought*, edited by Anne Waters (Malden, MA: Blackwell, 2004), 53.

175. Vine Deloria, Jr., *Indian Education in America* (Boulder, Colorado: The American Indian Science & Engineering Society, 1991), 10.

176. Charles Sanders Peirce, Collected Papers of Charles Sanders Peirce edited by Charles Hartshorne and Paul Weiss (Bristol, England: Thoemmes Press, 1998), volume 6, paragraph 104.

177. Ibid., paragraphs 155-157.

178. Peirce, "The Law of Mind," volume 6, paragraph 142.

179. Deloria, 11.

180. Ibid.,, 22.

181. *Smoke Signals*, 29

182. Maureen E. Smith, "Crippling the Spirit, Wounding the Soul: Native American Spiritual and Religious Suppression," in *American Indian Thought*, 117.

183. Deloria, 14.

184. Ibid., 14.

185. Peirce, volume 6, paragraphs 452-466. The essay is called, "A Neglected Argument for the Reality of God," the first section of which is entitled "Musement."

186. Deloria, 15

187. *Smoke Signals*, 167.

188. Deloria, 23.

7 | Bad Men at Play: On the Banality of Goodness in *Unforgiven*

189. A general discussion of the Primal Scene occurs in chapter IV of "From the History of Infantile Neurosis" in volume seventeen of, *The Standard Edition of the Complete Psychological Works of Sigmund Freud*, translated by James Strachey in collaboration

with Anna Freud, assisted by Alix Strachey and Alan Tyson, Volume XVII (1917-1919)(London: Hogarth Press, 1973), 29-47. 188. Žižek, *Everything You Always Wanted to Know about Lacan (But Were Afraid to Ask Hitchcock)* (New York: Verso, 2002), 235.

190. Žižek, *Everything You Always Wanted to Know about Lacan* (But Were Afraid to Ask Hitchcock) (New York: Verso, 2002), 235.

191. Hitchcock says to Peter Bogdonovich, "I believe in pure cinema." He goes on to say, "I think montage is the essential thing in a motion picture." Hitchcock describes the experiment by the Russian director Pudovkin who showed audiences the face of an actor, then a coffin, then the identical image of the same actor and a young woman. What the audience sees in the expression of the actor is very different in the two cases. The generating a specific response from the audience by means of a series of images on the screen is what Hitchcock means by "pure cinema." Peter Bognonovich, *Who the Devil Made It: Conversations with Legendary Film Directors* (New York: Ballantine Books, 1997), 476.

192. The idea of Eastwood's characters having some secret connection with the real of the immortals connects with the very nature of the medium of film itself, since on film, actors are, as it were, immortalized, taken out of time, at least in the contexts of the films in which they star. I owe this insight to Richard McClelland, commenting on an early draft of this paper.

193. Johan Huizinga, *Homo Ludens* (Boston, The Beacon Press, 1950), i.

194. Peter French, in his *Cowboy Metaphysics: Ethics and Death in Westerns* (New York: Roman & Littlefield, 1997), focuses his analysis of the Westerner on the division between the Christianized Easterners and the un-Christianized Westerner. He associates Easterners not just with being Christianized, but also with being feminized: "A rising tide of civilizing and Christianizing not only was led by women, but threatened to wash away the very activitiesand beliefs that men held to be their special domain, what they cared most about" (15). I read Eastwood's treatment of the Westerners in *Unforgiven* as trying to make problematic any simple dichotomy of Eastern=bad or feminine and Western=good or masculine (or vice versa).

195. *Homo Ludens*, 8.

196. Christopher Frayling, *Sergio Leone: Something to Do with Death* (New York: Faber and Faber, 2000), 273.

197. French calls this "deep play." As he says, "I define 'deep play' as any activity in which the stakes are so high that it is irrational for anyone to engage in it." *Cowboy Metaphysics*, 111.

198. Slavoj Žižek, *The Art of the Ridiculous Sublime: On David Lynch's Lost Highway* (Seattle: University of Washington Press, 2000), 13.

199. Henry David Thoreau, *Walden, or, Life in the Woods* (New York: Vintage Books/The Library of America Edition, 1991), 9 (Ch. 1, par. 9).

200. I owe considerable thanks to Richard McClelland and Brian Clayton for their many comments on an earlier draft of this paper.

Conclusions

201. Derrida, "The Law of Genre," 61.
202. Plato, *Symposium*, 211b-211c.

Index

40 Acres and a Mule – 67-68
Abrams, Jerold J. - 152
Abyss – 65
Adams, Evan – 110
Aeschylus – 36-37
Aftab, Kaleem – 153
Agathon – xi
Alexie, Sherman – 111, 113, 123, 156
Alienation – 39, 52, 54, 60-61, 116
Allegory – 98-99
Allegory of the Cave, the - 11
Altman, Robert – v, 151
America – 3-6, 15, 19-22, 24, 31, 76, 111, 124, 137, 143
American exceptionalism – 5
American mythos – 5
Antigone – 3
Anxiety – 12-13, 15, 34, 49, 50, 54, 60, 93
Apollo – 35-36, 38
Apollodorus – xi
Aristophanes – xi
Aristotle – 6, 30, 34, 64-65, 76, 103, 105, 148-49, 152
Art – iii, 9, 27, 32, 36, 44-45, 66, 81-82, 84, 86-92, 94, 96, 103-05, 135, 143, 154
Augenblick – 9
Augustine – 20, 102, 156
Auteur – 143-44
Awakenings – 112
Bad conscience – 54
Bad faith – 54, 148
Badiou, Alain – 9, 18, 148
Banality of Goodness – 127, 140
Bardem, Javier – xi, 25
Bargen, Daniel von – 26
Barrett, James R. – 154
Barthes, Roland – 60
Beach, Adam – 110
Beatty, Warren - vi
Bedard, Irene – 123
Bellini, Cal, - 113
Benedek, Patrick – 17
Bible, The – 37
Bohne, Bruce – 24
Bolton, John – 152

Bonanza- vii
Borde & Chaumoton – 60, 151-52
Bourgeois – vii, 39, 53-54, 60, 67, 135, 140
Brandon, Henry – 28
Bridges, Jeff – 18
Brodkin, Karen – 154
Brolin, Josh – 29
Bronson, Charles – 138
Brooklyn – 67
Butch Cassidy and the Sundance Kid – x
Cage, Nicolas – xi, 3
Cajete, Gregory – 117, 157
Campbell, Rob – 132
Camus, Albert – 34, 149
Capitalism – iii, 19, 20, 67, 72, 84, 88-89, 102, 137, 139-40, 151
Cardinale, Claudia – 139
Catharsis – 65
Cavell, Marc – 25
Cavell, Stanley – 110, 156
Chartier, Jean-Paul – 151
Cheyenne – 113, 138-40
Chief Dan George – 113
Christianity – iii
Christie, Julie – vi
Christopher, Nicholas – 151
Chuck D – 73
Civil War – 67, 112
Clans – 119
Clooney, George – 26
Cobb, Randall "Tex" – 7
Coen brothers, the – xi, 14, 18, 23-24, 26-27, 148-49
Coen, Ethan – 3, 18, 23, 28, 147-48
Coeur d'Alene Indians - 110
Cohen, Ted – 12, 13, 148
Comedy – vi, xi, 3, 6-7, 15, 20, 22, 83, 112, 148
Commodity Economics – 71-73, 115-16
Conard, Mark – i, 152
Conceptual Tools – 129-31
Conversation – 96-98, 100, 102, 112, 139, 144, 145
Cool Hand Luke – 25-26
Costner, Kevin – 112-13
Dances with Wolves – 112
Dante – 6, 13-14, 17, 18, 20, 148
Darwin, Charles – 82
Death – xi, 29, 33-34, 38, 39-40, 43, 51, 55, 57-58, 62, 65-66, 99, 101, 131-32, 140, 142, 150, 158

Deconstruction – iii, 61, 144
Deloria, Vine – 109, 117, 122, 125, 157
Democracy – iii, 19
Dennett, Daniel – 56, 152
Derrida, Jacques – iii, iv, v, ix, x, 27, 60, 143, 147, 149
Detour – 53
Dewey, John – 67, 82, 88-90, 99, 102, 110, 154-55
Dillahunt, Garret – 24
Dionysus – 35, 36
Do the Right Thing – 81, 153
Doppelgänger – 62-63
Dorsey, Marc – 67
Dostoyevsky, Fyodor – 49
Double Indemnity – 53
Double-Consciousness – 72, 73, 75, 79
Dreams – 6, 16, 18-19, 22, 45, 62, 148
Du Bois, W.E.B. – 72-73, 75, 153
Dunaway, Faye – 53
Durgnat, Raymond – 151
Eastwood, Clint – i, vii, xii, 127, 129-32, 137-38, 142-43, 158
Eaton, Michael – 152
Eliot, T. S. – 54
Emerson, Ralph Waldo – 3, 5, 29, 110, 147, 149
Enlightenment, The – iii, 35-37, 49
Eros – 115
Ethics of Anguish – 75
Euripides – 36
Europe – 15, 20, 37, 49
Event – 9, 10, 18, 51, 90
Evil – 17, 26, 28, 33, 59, 61, 64, 70, 77, 81, 131, 140, 148
Existentialism – 35, 49, 52
Eyre, Chris – xii, 109, 113, 143
Fargo – 5, 23-24, 26
Farmer, Gary – 110
Farrakhan, Louis – 80
Fate – 29, 40, 50-51, 91, 104, 131
Film noir – 27, 49-53, 55, 60, 76, 151-53
Finnerty, Warren – 25
Fish, Stanley – viii, 147
Fisher, Francis – 133
Flory, Dan – 76, 153
Foley, Neil – 154
Fonda, Henry – 136, 138
Ford, John – vii, viii, 28, 40, 134, 136
Foreign Correspondent – 61
Forms –10, 11, 36, 50, 72, 76, 116, 121, 127-28, 133, 143

Forsythe, William – 7
Foucault, Michel – 60, 102, 156
France – 49-50, 60
Frank, Nino – 151
Fränkel, Hermann – 32, 149
Freedom – vii, 5, 16, 18, 22, 40, 44, 59, 99, 135, 137, 142
Freeman, Morgan – 135
French, Peter – 38-39, 150, 158
Freud, Sigmund – 13, 16, 49-51, 53, 60-62, 64, 66, 129-30, 135, 151-52, 157-58
Genre – iv, v, vi, vii, ix, x, xi, xii, 7, 27, 49, 50, 53, 110, 131, 134, 143-44, 147, 149, 151, 159
Germany – 49
Gifts – 71, 72, 114-16, 122-23
Giuffrie, Aldo – 132
God – viii, 14, 53, 86, 91, 135, 142, 153, 157
Goodman, John – 7, 18
Greek tragedy – 29, 31, 36, 41, 57, 66
Guilt – x, 15, 42, 57, 59-60
Hackman, Gene – 136
Hamartia – 31, 57
Harding, Elizabeth – 52
Harrelson, Woody – 33
Harris, Keith M. – 153-54
Hawks, Howard – 53
Heaps - v
Heidegger, Martin – 9, 49, 73, 148
Heraclitus of Ephesus – 32, 33, 149
Hermeneutics – 53
Hill, George Roy – x
Hillerman, John – 61
Hitchcock, Alfred – 60-61, 92, 130, 156, 158
Hollywood – 43, 50, 53, 60, 113, 155
Homo Faber – 137
Homo Ludens – 137, 158
Hubris – 28-31, 45, 57
Huizinga, Johan – 137, 139, 158
Humor – 11, 25, 114, 121
Hunter, Jeffrey – 28
Hurston, Zora Neale – 73, 153
Huston, John – 53, 55, 152
Hyde, Lewis – 71, 115-16, 153, 157
Ideology – 89, 95
Identity – 5, 7-10, 16-17, 19, 37, 58, 109-10, 119, 143
Ingberg, Affi – 153
Interpretation – iii, 6, 14, 16, 54, 75, 82, 93, 99, 102, 129-30, 151, 154
Invagination – ix
Irony – 19, 23-24, 76, 92-93, 143, 153

James, Anthony – 132
James, Henry – 27, 77, 149
James, Raymond – 67
James, William – 110
Jameson, Fredric – 151
Jesus – 37
Jokes – 11-13, 148
Jones, Gene – 34
Jones, Tommy Lee – 24
Kairos Time – 69, 102-03
Kant, Immanuel – 88-89, 102, 152, 154
Kavanagh, James – 152
Keitel, Harvey – 70
Kierkegaard, Soren – 49
Kitei, Lynne Dumin – xi, 21
Kronos Time – 69, 102-03
Ku klux klan – 24
Ladd, Diane – 55
Lakota Sioux Indians – 112
Law – vii, x, 4, 7, 10, 26-28, 35, 40, 43, 67, 68, 74, 89-90, 98-99, 117-18, 132, 135-38
Law of Genre – iv, ix, 27, 143-44, 147, 149, 159
Lee, Spike – 67-68, 70, 74, 75-78, 80-82, 143, 153-54
Leone, Sergio – 131-32, 134, 136-37, 158
Levine, Anna – 133
Lindo, Delroy – 70
Lipsitz, George – 154
Little Big Man - 44, 113
Logos – 115
Los Angeles – 57-58
Love – v, 4, 9-11, 17, 19, 52-53, 60, 62, 64-66, 77-78, 80-82, 86, 128, 130, 142-43
Lyotard, Jean-François – iii, 74, 84, 147, 152-54
Macdonald, Kelly – 34
Malcolm X – 67, 79
Man Who Shot Liberty Valance, The – 40, 134
Marriage – vi, vii, 4, 7, 10, 21
Marshall, Penny – 112
Marx, Karl – 53, 60, 66
Massood, Paula J. – 153
McCabe & Mrs. Miller – v
McCarthy, Cormac – 23, 28, 149-50
McCrea, Joel – 61
McDormand, Frances – 13, 24
McGuffin – 137
McKelly, James C. – 153
McRae, Tony – 151
Melville, Herman – 28, 70

Metanarrative – iii, iv
Metaphor – ix, 3, 7, 38, 53
Metaphysics – 16, 18, 38, 60, 88, 102, 114, 117, 127, 148, 150, 154, 158
Miles, Elaine – 113
Milton, John – viii
Misé en scene – 127-28
Moby Dick – 28, 70
Modernism – iii
Monster – 29, 149
Morality – 40, 53, 88-89
Mucci, David – 132
My Darling Clementine – 136
Myth – 22, 86, 109, 131
Naremore, James – 151
Nash, Roderick Frazier – 37, 150
Nation of Islam – 80
Native American – 72, 109-10, 112, 114, 119, 121, 143, 156, 157
Nature – 4, 28, 31, 35, 37-38, 89, 90, 110, 116-18, 128-29, 131, 135-36
Neo-genre – ix, x, xi
Newman, Paul – 25
Nicholson, Jack – 52
Nicomachean Ethics – 30, 34, 103, 149
Nietzsche, Friedrich – 16, 26, 36, 37, 39, 45, 49, 53, 60, 66, 94, 148, 150
Nostalgia – 51, 54, 151
Nuclear war – 49, 50
Nunn, Bill – 81
Oedipus – 29, 57, 58-60, 62-64, 152
Once Upon a Time in the West – 134, 136-138
Oppression – 12, 15, 49-50, 67, 69, 75, 79, 137
Optative – 3, 5
Oracle of Delphi – 29-30, 57
Out of the Past – 53
Outlaw, the – x, 3-4, 7- 8, 10, 17, 40, 46
Palmer, Belinda - 55
Paradise Lost – viii, 147
Paradox – iv, v, 54, 65, 77
Particulars – 8, 50, 119, 128-29
Pee Wee Love – 70
Peirce, Charles Sanders – 77, 80-82, 110, 117-18, 121-22, 124, 127, 154, 157
Penn, Arthur – 44, 113
Penumbra – v, vi, ix, x, xi, 77
Phifer, Mekhi – 69
Philosophy – vi, ix, 16, 24, 32-33, 49-50, 52, 60, 76, 81, 88-99, 105, 109-10, 117, 121-22, 124, 126-28, 130, 131, 137-38, 142-44
Phoenix, AZ – 110, 112, 120
Pistilli, Luigi – 132

Plato – xi, 11, 22, 44, 103, 127, 143, 145, 147-48, 155-56, 159
Play – 5, 45, 46, 49, 76, 136-41,158
Polanski, Roman – xi, 51, 53, 55, 66, 143, 152-53
Polysemous – 14-17
Postmodernism – iii, 144, 151-52
Potlatch – 72, 117
Power – iii, x, 10, 28-31, 38-39, 50, 53, 56, 58-59, 62-66, 69, 71, 74, 86, 109, 118, 122, 127, 136
Pragmatic – 76, 109, 113, 117
Pragmatism – 110, 126, 156
Primal scene – 129, 130, 157
Public Enemy – 73
Pulver, Andrew – 18
Pure cinema – 130, 158
Puritanism – 137
Racism – viii, 67-68, 70, 72-73, 75, 78-79, 153
Rank, Otto – 62
Reagan, Ronald – 4, 8
Reality – 9, 11, 16, 18, 39, 52, 74-75, 88, 98, 104-05, 117, 119, 127-28, 157
Repetition – iv, 15, 51, 61, 63, 65, 147
Ricoeur, Paul – 53, 151
Robards, Jason – 136
Roediger, David – 154
Rorty, Richard – 60, 76, 152
Rosenberg, Stuart – 25
Rothenberg, Paula S. – 153
Russell, Bertrand – v, 147
Sarris, Andrew – 152
Sartre, Jean Paul – 49, 54, 66, 95-96, 148
Schrader, Paul – 49, 151
Scotoma – 55-57, 59, 66
Scott, Ridley – x, 113
Searchers, The – vii, 28, 136
Seeger, Pete – 3, 4, 147
Sesslen, George – 10, 147-48
Sherman, William Tecumseh – 67
Shetley, Vernon – 152
Siegal, Don – 137
Silver, Alain – 151-52
Sin – viii, 14, 17, 20, 71, 147
Sinister – 59
Slotkin, Richard – 109, 114, 156-57
Smith, Maureen E. – 121, 157
Smoke Signals – xii, 109-11, 113-14, 120, 122, 126, 156-57
Socrates – xi, 36, 103, 143
Sophocles – 36-37

Sorcerer's Apprentice, The – 28
Sorites Paradox – iv, v, 77
Sperber, Murray – 152
St. John, Michelle – 113
Sublime – 36, 64-65, 128, 152, 158
Symposium – xi, 143, 147, 159
Taylor, Regina – 70
Tiresias - 59
Tenderness – 10, 12-13, 21, 22, 40, 78, 134
The Big Sleep – 53
The Good, the Bad, the Ugly – 132, 137
The Linguistic Turn – 60, 152
The Maltese Falcon – 53, 151
The Man Who Shot Liberty Valance – 40, 134
Thelma & Louise – x, 113
Theory – iii, ix, 11, 27, 87, 149, 154
Thoreau, Henry David – 38, 110, 140, 150, 158
Time – 4, 9, 17, 60, 69, 72-74, 84, 86, 88, 98, 100, 102-03, 118, 125, 148
Tocqueville, Alexis de – 5
Tourneur, Jacques – 53
Towne, Robert – 53, 55, 152
Tragedy – xi, 29-31, 36, 41, 51, 57-59, 64-66, 76, 150, 152
Truth – iii, 4, 13, 22, 40, 54, 57, 60, 66, 86, 100, 121, 123, 138, 144, 148, 153
U. S. Constitution – 35-36
Uberty - 22
Ulmer, Edgar – 53
Uncanny – 61-63, 152
Unforgiven – vii, xii, 127-32, 136-37, 141, 158
Unger, Peter – 79, 147
Universals – 8
Ursini, James – 151
Vagueness – v, vi, 147
Venetian blinds – xi, 52-53, 58
Vietnam war – 30, 60
Violence – vii, viii, xii, 19, 40, 49-51, 67, 76, 109-11, 114, 129-31, 134-36, 143, 156
Virgil – 18
Washington, Isaiah – 70
Wayne, John – vii, 29, 40, 124, 136
Wentz, Jaime – 133
West, Cornell – 79, 110, 154, 156
Western, the – v, vii, x, xii, 7, 23, 27-28, 38, 49, 109-10, 112, 131, 134-37, 143, 150, 158
White, Steve – 70
Wilder, Billy – 53
Wildness – 7, 37, 38-40, 134-36
Wilson, Trey – 19
Winthrop, John – 5, 147

Wisdom – 4, 17, 30, 32-33, 36, 38, 41-42, 44, 45, 65-66, 81, 117, 119-121, 126-27, 144
Woodward, Morgan – 25
Yeats, William Butler – 17, 44-45, 150
Young, Burt – 52
Žižek, Slavoj – 61, 74, 99, 112-13, 130, 140, 152-53, 155-56, 158
Zwerling, Darnell – 55

www.ingramcontent.com/pod-product-compliance
Lightning Source LLC
Chambersburg PA
CBHW021156160426
43194CB00007B/764